Scraping the Surface

Objects in Mirror
are Stranger
Than They Appear

Cut!

Scraping the Surface

Objects in Mirror are Stranger Than They Appear

Lyle Victor Albert

Prairie Play Series: 19/ Series Editor, Diane Bessai

© Copyright Lyle Victor Albert 2000

Production Rights: Rights to amateur productions of this play may be obtained through Playwrights' Union of Canada, 54 Wolseley St., 2nd Fl. Toronto, Ontario, Canada, M5T 1A5. Rights to any other productions, theatrical or otherwise, may be obtained through the playwright in care of Crescent Moon Productions, Box 572, Radium Hot Springs, British Columbia, Canada, V0A 1M0.

Canadian Cataloguing in Publication Data

Albert, Lyle Victor.
  Scraping the surface

  (Prairie play series ; 19)
  Plays.
  ISBN 1-896300-33-2

  I. Title. II. Series.
PS8551.L3773S37 2000   C812',54   C00-910685-5
PR9199.3.A3645S37 2000

Editor for the Press: Lynne Van Luven
Cover design: Bob Young
Cover photograph: Ryan Bavin

Canadian   Patrimoine
Heritage   canadien

THE CANADA COUNCIL | LE CONSEIL DES ARTS
FOR THE ARTS | DU CANADA
SINCE 1957 | DEPUIS 1957

NeWest Press acknowledges the support of the Canada Council for the Arts for our publishing program. We also acknowledge the financial support of the Government of Canada through the Book Publishing Industry Development Program (BPIDP) for our publishing activities.

NeWest Press
201-8540-109 Street
Edmonton, Alberta T6G 1E6
(780) 432-9427
www.newestpress.com

1 2 3 4 5 04 03 02 01 00

PRINTED AND BOUND IN CANADA

Contents

.

This collection of plays is
dedicated to Jace van der Veen.

I met Jace van der Veen in the fall of 1982. He was the
newly appointed Artistic Director of Northern Light Theatre in
Edmonton, and I was a second-year University of Alberta undergrad-
uate with a mess of a play called *The Prairie Church of Buster
Galloway*. All dramatics aside, little did I know that meeting would
change my life.

On paper it didn't work. Jace was urbane and sophisticated, and
I was a farm kid writing ... well, rural. But he decided to include my
play in his first season at Northern Light Theatre. At the first reading,
it really didn't work. The play was misshapen, unfocused and des-
tined to become an "experiment." But Jace didn't give up. His skills
as a director and a dramaturge challenged me to constantly clarify,
to find the dramatic action and to tell a story that people would care
about. I would cringe every time Jace presented me with his notes,
which were not in the form of 'this is right or this is wrong', but as
questions. These were questions that I didn't necessarily have to
answer, but I needed a hell of good reason if I didn't.

The success of *The Prairie Church of Buster Galloway* gave me
the confidence I needed. Like everyone involved in the production, I
did my best. And Jace van der Veen brought out the best in all of us.
More important, we became friends. Although he never directed any
of my other plays, he helped direct my life by his friendship, his gen-
erosity of spirit and his mischievous nature that sometimes pushed a

little further than you wanted to go. "Why not?" and "What if?" were his invitations to life, and you would be a fool not to accept.

Several years ago, Jace moved from Edmonton to the Netherlands, the land of his birth. Last year I had the good fortune to visit him. We had a wonderful time. But Jace couldn't help directing even as we walked down the street. He chided me for walking with my head down. "Vic, why do you always have your head down when you walk? Look up, pay attention to what's around you. Imagine yourself sitting in the air." It was good advice, I saw a lot more of Amsterdam and managed not to trip over my own two feet.

Sadly, Jace van der Veen passed away in July after a brief illness. It was a shock to see a life so vibrant taken away too soon. To say I'll miss Jace hardly sums up what he meant to my life and to the thousands of others who had the good fortune to know him. But I know Jace is on another adventure. He's sitting in the air, exploring the Universe and having a great time.

Lyle Victor Albert
August 15, 2000

Introduction

If you travel northeast of Alberta's capital city of Edmonton, through the rolling countryside where fields of Canola and barley flourish in the summer, past the lakes and resort areas, after about 260 kilometres you will come to the shores of Jessie Lake and the town of Bonnyville, "heart of the lakeland," population 5,500.

There, just one block off Main Street, in a converted gymnasium next to the town's consolidated high school, you will find the Lyle Victor Albert Centre, named in tribute to one of the community's successful native sons. It's an ordinary-looking building that seats about 200 people; it's not the Palladium or the Coliseum, but, aside from the hockey arena and the high school gym, it's one of the town's best-used public spaces.

However, if you had been in Bonnyville on March 2, 1985, the Lyle Victor Albert Centre would not have been big enough for the crowd of 400 gathered to see the first local production of that native son's first play, *The Prairie Church of Buster Galloway*. The enthusiastic audience had to be accommodated next door, in the new gym, where the playwright's parents, cousins, siblings, assorted town folks and a gaggle of his pals from the big smoke of Edmonton surged through the doors.

Everyone was delighted: not only had the baby who almost died a few days after birth managed to grow into an irrepressible youth, a self-described "jumpy" with an unruly nimbus of strawberry-blond hair, he'd not let cerebral palsy stop him from doing what he wanted to do, whether it was riding a bicycle, driving a truck, going to college, drinking beer, studying English and drama at university, writing plays or getting up on a stage himself. In fact, ever since early childhood, Vic had lived his life as if to demonstrate that CP, a spastic paralysis that occurs from brain damage before or during birth, didn't define him.

Vic himself recalls the occasion as "one of the more memorable days of my life … It was a 'local boy makes good' thing: it was thrilling to come back and have something you've created, a story about where you grew up, for the folks you grew up with."

"I remember how proud he was," says Stephen Heatley, now a theatre instructor at the University of British Columbia. Back in the mid-eighties, Heatley was the artistic director at Theatre Network in Edmonton. "Everyone was there, and of course everyone knew him. And he was telling a story that belonged to those people."

Sometimes in a writer's life, private and public worlds mysteriously combine to result in that evanescent third thing, a creative expression, a work of art, that bridges the gap between self and other. It doesn't happen often and it doesn't happen without great struggle, even pain. But when work rooted in a playwright's core transcends personal chaos and speaks to everyone else, a momentary hush falls over an audience. During such a moment, there's a special "paying attention" that neither audience nor playwright ever forgets. Such was the feeling in Bonnyville's high school gym that night in early March, as the story of an elevator agent's trials captivated the crowd.

A similar transcendence occurs in both *Scraping the Surface* and *Objects in Mirror*, performance pieces in which Lyle Victor Albert, the basic human guy, becomes Vic the character becomes Vic the actor. Although humour is the base of both plays, it's comedy based on everyday experience and grounded in personal struggle. Director for both original productions was Richard Lett.

Stephen Heatley agrees that the power in both plays stems from the fact that "the character is the artist." Heatley recalls the young playwright learning how to type just after he got his first computer, finally being able to revise with ease. "He was just finding his feet and beginning to have the confidence to say, 'I'm an artist,' and expect to be taken seriously," Heatley recalls.

"When Vic first started writing, he wrote about things that any playwright growing up in rural Alberta would write about." But as he grew as an artist, Heatley says, Lyle Victor Albert had to come to grips with being a performer, and learn how to bring personal experience into his one-person plays.

"I remember what must have been a seminal experience, though I didn't realize it at the time," Heatley recalls. "He was our playwright in residence, and one day when we went out for lunch, Vic ordered soup. Afterwards he told me, 'That's the first time I've ever eaten a bowl of soup in public.' That was the thing that was fascinating: what the rest of us took for granted was high drama for Vic."

Brian Paisley of Victoria, the man responsible for launching Edmonton's renowned Fringe Festival in 1982, regrets that he "cannot take credit for discovering" Lyle Victor Albert.

"But I do recall that *Prairie Church* was a huge hit. I became aware of Vic's active mind and great sense of humour at the same time as I realized he had CP. For some, it was difficult to reconcile. You either had to go with the whole package or back away."

During the heady days of the Edmonton arts scene in the 1980s, Paisley was part of a large, fluid group of writers and actors who congregated in the bar at the Strathcona Hotel on Whyte Avenue to celebrate successes and drown sorrows.

"Vic fell into the gang at the Strath quite naturally," Paisley says. "I think he had the same semi-cynical way of looking at things we all did. And in the theatre world, everyone's a bit of an eccentric, so most people never thought twice about his CP. That's part of him, it's part of his skewed sense of reality."

Nancy Mairs, an American author who was diagnosed with multiple sclerosis at the age of 29, writes eloquently and forthrightly about living with what society sees as a "handicap." Mairs prefers to call herself a "cripple" and notes that no one can divorce herself from her body, however much she would like to. In *Waist High in the World: A Life Among the Nondisabled*, Mair writes: "Who would I be if I didn't have MS? Literally, no body. I am not "Nancy + MS," and no simple subtraction can render me whole. Nor do I contain MS, like a tumor that might be sliced out … I would be diminished, even damaged, without MS." She maintains that she would have been a writer even if she had not developed multiple sclerosis, "but I could not conceivably have become the writer I am." One imagines that Lyle Victor Albert would have become a writer even if he hadn't developed CP, but one suspects that at least some of his subject material might have been handled differently.

Lyle Victor Albert's "skewed" vision found a natural outlet in fringe theatre, with its mandate of pushing boundaries and introducing audiences to plays in progress written from a variety of perspectives. *Cut!*, first published in 1986 by NeWest Press in *Five From the Fringe*, edited by Nancy Bell, showcases Vic's ability to imagine marginalized characters—specifically those excised from famous plays who must confront their own resulting ignominious lack of celebrity—with both compassion and humour. The audience soon comes to see why Hamlet's brother Clyde treads no boards, why Tennessee Williams had to get rid of Stanley Kowalski's mother, why Oscar Wilde cut Fiddleditch, an overly obsequious butler, from ALL his plays, and why Sophocles was right to delete Nippletitus, Oedipus's histrionic sister, from his great work, *Oedipus Rex*. At the same time, viewers understand and relate to these characters' peevish umbrage—with the possible exception of the weepy old man (first played by Vic himself) who shuffles on stage at the very end of the play.

If Lyle Victor Albert is simply, as Brian Paisley suggests, an Everyman with a tilt, his hard-earned equanimity probably stems from to his upbringing in a solid rural family of French/Irish Catholic extraction.

"I'm the youngest of eight (five sisters, two brothers) ... I think growing up on a farm in a large family gave me a sense of humour, which I hope has served me well in my writing," Albert has written.

"Much of my humour comes out of growing up with cerebral palsy and seeing the humour in any given situation. That's not to say it hasn't been difficult at times, but a good laugh can smooth out a lot of rough spots. I credit that attitude to my parents, who treated me like any another kid and refused to indulge me in self-pity—even when I so did want to be indulged."

Unlike Canadian playwright David Freeman, who also has cerebral palsy and whose first play, *Creeps*, (produced at Toronto's Factory Theatre Lab in 1971) was set in a sheltered workshop, Vic has been reluctant to write about his own physical difficulties. In fact, when he began writing, he made a conscious decision "not to ever write about CP. I didn't want the 'disabled writer' tag," he says.

"Freeman wrote *Creeps*, and it was a good play and had a lot of success, but it sort of defined him after that. I really wanted to avoid that."

However, in a production at the Edmonton Fringe in 1984, Vic himself played Tom, the spastic character in *Creeps* who realizes "there's no time left," and eventually finds the courage to leave the sheltered workshop.

"I have a funny story about that," Lyle Victor Albert reports with delight. "I didn't actually hear this, but a friend told me that after the play was over, a member of the audience said, 'that was a good show, but the red-headed guy wasn't very convincing.' " It's the kind of absurdist situation—actuality being mistaken for artifice—that delights him.

Despite Vic's attempts to avoid it, in the mid-nineties, his disablity became his material almost by accident: "A friend of mine, Richard Lett, asked me to write and perform a 15-minute monologue for the Vancouver Men's Festival he was producing. It was a one-shot deal, so I figured, 'what the hell?' I wrote a piece about shaving from the perspective of someone with CP.

"I had no illusions about performing it other than that one night, but the audience reaction was quite overwhelming. I figured I was on to something, so I expanded the piece into an hour, then into a two-act version."

Given the success of the direct-address monologue in *Scraping the Surface*, Lyle Victor Albert next tackled the subject of moving on, in geography and relationships, in "*Objects in Mirror*," an even riskier delving into personal material written out of the rawness of a failed relationship.

"It was harder to write, it went a little deeper, and looked at a really sensitive area," the playwright says.

While he's still casting about for new subjects today, Vic doesn't seem to be able to stop shaving. In the past six years, he has performed "*Scraping the Surface*" more than 700 times, throughout Canada and in Ireland, Scotland and England, making him the most publicly well-shaven playwright in North America.

On April 1, 1995, he even took the show out to the Lyle Victor Albert Centre in Bonnyville, where he reports that it was a huge success, "even though my knees were shaking so bad I thought I was gonna fall down." This fall, he's going on tour in the United States with *Scraping the Surface*, starting with a production at the Kennedy Centre in Washington, D.C. Jumpy or not, the Boy from Bonnyville keeps moving along.

Lynne Van Luven
Victoria, B.C
July 28, 2000

Playography

OTHER PLAYS:

Prairie Church of Buster Galloway, First produced 1983, Northern
  Light Theatre, Edmonton
Cut! First produced 1985, Edmonton Fringe Festival
White on White, First produced 1985, Theatre Network, Edmonton;
  workshopped at Stratford
The Big Sell, First produced 1986 by Theatre Network, Fort
  McMurray
Ba Ha Ha, First produced 1987, Edmonton Fringe Festival
Waves, First produced 1989, Alberta Theatre Projects, Calgary
Wheelie, First produced 1988, Chinook Theatre
Scraping The Surface, First produced 1995, Vancouver Men's Fest
Objects in Mirror, First produced 1997, Saskatoon Fringe Festival

AWARDS:

Elizabeth Sterling Haynes Award, 1996
Jessie Richardson Award, 1997
Alberta Culture Playwriting Award, 1986 for *Cut!,*
  1982 for *The Prairie Church of Buster Galloway*

PUBLISHED PLAYS:

The Prairie Church of Buster Galloway, New Works Anthology,
  Playwrights Union of Canada, 1987
Cut!, Five From the Fringe, NeWest Press, 1986

Tanya Ryga as Nippletitus and Larry Reese as Clyde in *Cut!*
Photo by Gorm Larsen, *The Edmonton Sun.*

Cut!

CUT! was first performed by Limited Time Offer Theatre, Edmonton, at the fourth Fringe Theatre Event, Old Strathcona, August 21, 1985, with the following cast:

Clyde: *Larry Reese*

Fiddleditch: *George Highsmith*

Nippletitus: *Tanya Ryga*

Mrs. Kowalski: *Barbara Reese*

Joey: *Eric Kramer*

Directed by Wendell Smith

Cut! was translated into French by Theatre Français d'Edmonton for productions in Edmonton, Paris, and Luxembourg in October 1986.

Scene One

An almost-bare stage, except for a couch and chair: a celestial waiting room with an illusion of infinite space.

The sound of a man weeping intermittently is heard offstage throughout the play. Sometimes it is soft and at other times it is very loud. Clyde enters—an Elizabethan dressed all in black. He has an unhappy disposition. The weeping suddenly gets very loud. Clyde tries his best to ignore it, but he cannot.

Clyde: Oh, will you please be quiet. Silence. Shut up. *Slowly.* All right, let us see. "To be or not to be" no, "To be or why not," "Why not to be" no, no, "To be or maybe" no, "To be or not to be" no ... yes, yes that's it. "To be or not to be—that is the question. Whether 'tis nobler in the mind to a noble mind," no, no, no that's not it. Stupid, stupid! *He massages his temples.* Oh, why can I not remember, after all, it was mine. It was mine. Why did he take it away from me? He had no right. Elizabethan bastard. *A loud sob offstage.* Shut up! Shut up! I can't stand it, I can not stand it.

An elderly Victorian butler enters. He walks slowly and speaks softly.

Fiddleditch: Sir:

Clyde: *Not looking at him.* What is it Fiddleditch?

Fiddleditch: Still practising I see ... sir?

Clyde: Well, what is it?

Fiddleditch: I have a message.

Clyde: A message?! A message to say that I have been put here in wrongful exile … yes, that's it. I'm free. Freedom at last. That's what is says, doesn't it Fiddleditch?

Fiddleditch: Well … no, sir. The message is to inform you that you are part of the welcoming committee today, for the new arrival. Sorry, sir.

Clyde: Surely you jest. I, on the welcoming committee? Impossible.

Fiddleditch: I have the notification here, sir. Sorry, sir.

Clyde: *He takes the note.* Why must you always apologize.

Fiddleditch: Apologize, sir? I don't know. Sor … sorry.

Clyde: And why don't you speak up, you always talk in a maddening hush.

Fiddleditch: I can't help it sir. It is my character.

Clyde: *Reading note.* This is an outrage. I refuse to stoop so low.

Fiddleditch: We all have to play our part sir.

Clyde: Yes, but I? I, Clyde, the prince. Why should I waste my time greeting some miserable misfit of a character who should never have been conceived of in the first place. No. It is beneath my station.

Fiddleditch: We were all freshly cut at one time, and speaking for myself, sir, I was glad for the support given by the welcoming party.

Clyde: You would be. *Pause.* Well, who is it?

Fiddleditch: All I know is that he's a modern.

Clyde: But of course. That's all we get nowadays. You would think they bred with each other.

Fiddleditch: Perhaps. It is the fashion, sir.

Clyde: Who else is on the welcoming party today?

Fiddleditch: There's Nippletitus …

Clyde: Oh yes, Nippletitus, the Greek. Well, this may not be so insufferable after all … All right, I'll do it.

Fiddleditch: And Mrs. Kowalski.

Clyde: Oh my curséd soul, that bitch?

Fiddleditch: You know her?

Clyde: Only by reputation. It's no wonder she's here and not her son.

Fiddleditch: You mean Stanley?

Clyde: Who else would I be referring to? Could you imagine if she had remained in. What an outrage. It would have made a mere marginal play absolutely dreadful.

Fiddleditch: I've met her once. She's such a bully.

Clyde: But of course, she's American. A clear example of the undesirable modern.

Fiddleditch: I was given such a gentle disposition, I can't take her bullying.

Clyde: Well, if that mindless theatrical whore bothers you today, she will have to answer to me.

Fiddleditch: Thank you, sir. That is very kind of you. *He starts to leave. Pauses.*

Clyde: *Thinking.* All right…. Whether 'tis nobler in the mind…

Fiddleditch: Sir?

Clyde: What is it now Fiddleditch?

Fiddleditch: I am going to prepare cucumber sandwiches for the new arrival and was wondering if you might care for one. They're made by my very own hands.

Clyde: No, no, no I would not like a cucumber sandwich made by your very own hands. You ask me that every day, and every day I give you the same answer. NO! Now be gone you rogue and peasant slave.

Fiddleditch hurries offstage. Clyde thinks.

Clyde: Rogue and peasant slave? … Yes, yes, I rather like that. I do believe that was mine too. "O what a rogue and peasant slave am I! …" *He tries to continue but cannot.* Damn you. Damn you. You think you're so smart. You had no right to cut me out and throw me on the trash heap like so many convoluted plots. And to give it all to my morose brother. You will get yours, you just wait. HACK! HACK!

At that moment a young, voluptuous girl enters. She wears a Classical Greek chiton.

Nippletitus: Oh good sir of pious intent, why so loud?

Clyde: It is none of your concern.

Nippletitus: Your words ring in my ears, by Athena.

Clyde: My dear lady, it is called projection.

Nippletitus: I know of what you speak. I, as a Greek, know all about the gods' gift of projection. *Pause.* Still depressed. Do not despair, you'll get over it, I did.

Clyde: You've had a longer time than I to reconcile yourself to your fate.

Nippletitus: A man here for less than four hundred years should not talk about the length of time for resolve. Hear me, I speak with knowledge of many, many centuries on this place. I have suppressed my laments long ago, Clyde.

Clyde: PRINCE Clyde.

Nippletitus: Oh yes, Prince Clyde. Prince Clyde of Denmark.

Clyde: And you should know that they will find proof of my existence. The folio that is rightfully mine.

Nippletitus: You speak with the voice of a character so prideful.

Clyde: I beg your pardon.

Nippletitus: Hear me, hear me, hear me. Pride will be your downfall. Oh pride, wicked pride, awful pride, terrible pride, stupid pride. Your belief that you are above all others is wrong, wrong, wrong, wrong. The gods have laid their judgement upon you. The oracle at Dephi has spoken, and it says, "big deal."

Clyde: Spoken like a true Greek with bad translation.

Nippletitus: I'm proud to be a Greek.

Clyde: But nobody, nobody does *you* anymore, do they, my dear lady. All that *deus ex machina* nonsense.

Nippletitus: Oh Yeah? Well at least I know who wrote me! Maybe you're a Marlowe or a Jonson or a Simple Simon.

Clyde takes a deep breath. A nerve has been struck.

Nippletitus: We should not fight over things we cannot change. All is in the hands of Zeus, or whichever god is working today. We cannot change what the gods have ordained.

Clyde: You Greeks and your gods. What a quaint way of dismissing life's tragedies.

Nippletitus: Listen to the tale I have to tell. I have been betrayed too. I was cut from the great Greek play, *Oedipus the King*. I was his sister and I was to be his queen. How we could have loved. Night and day, day and night, night and day. Everywhere. In the kitchen, in the stables in the courtyard. Everywhere! He was so good … to me. But alas, it was not meant to be. Our mother Jocasta wanted him for herself, isn't that sick? So Sophocles married off my Oedipus to her, leaving me cut on the bedroom floor—unfulfilled. Oh woe, oh woe, oh woe.

Pause. Clyde tries to comfort her.

Clyde: Oh please, you do have my greatest sympathy.

Nippletitus: I do not need sympathy. We must resign ourselves to our fate, fate, fate.

Clyde: Of course. But perhaps we may go over it in more detail tonight. A walk, perhaps a fulfilling … talk. For my sake. What say you, dear Nippletitus?

Nippletitus: *Coyly.* Perhaps.

Fiddleditch returns carrying a plate of cucumber sandwiches. Right behind him is Mrs. Kowalski carrying a box. Fiddleditch stops abruptly, and Mrs. Kowalski nearly plows into him. She is middle-aged and loud.

Mrs. Kowalski: For crying out loud Fiddleditch, move it or get out of the way.

Fiddleditch: Sorry.

Mrs. Kowalski: You bet your ass you're sorry. You're the sorriest excuse for a character I ever saw.

Clyde: Ahh, yes, you must be Mrs. Kowalski. *Aside.* A woman by any other name would stand on all fours and give milk.

Mrs. Kowalski: Well, well, if it ain't black beauty. Don't tell me you're on the welcoming committee today.

Clyde: The pleasure is all yours.

Mrs. Kowalski: Learn your lines yet, Prince?

Clyde: Methinks, Mrs. Kowalski, you should return to that which is your nature and chew your cud.

Mrs. Kowalski moves towards Clyde. Nippletitus moves between them.

Nippletitus: Please, I wish you wouldn't fight, we should love and be loved.

Mrs. Kowalski: You Greeks know all about love don't you. Tramp!

Nippletitus: Such sour grapes.

Fiddleditch: Sir? *He offers Clyde a sandwich.*

Clyde: No! I have already told you Fiddleditch, I don't want any cucumber sandwiches. No one here wants, or likes, cucumber sandwiches, and here you are with a plate full of cucumber sandwiches!

Fiddleditch: I'm sorry, sir, but you know I can't help it; it is a great part of my character. Mr. Wilde never gave me much motivation, so I'm left with this … Perhaps the new arrival will enjoy them.

Clyde: We can always hope.

Mrs. Kowalski: All right, the new guy is going to be here soon. We got to get ready. *She reaches into the box and pulls out party hats and noise makers.* Here everybody, put these on.

Clyde: You are mad.

Mrs. Kowalski: Look it's not my idea, it comes from the top. They say that it's the welcoming committee's job to make the new arrival feel more welcome. So here, put 'em on.

Clyde: I will not.

Mrs. Kowalski: Look, black beauty, I didn't cart these down for nothing. Put it on, and take these.

They all reluctantly put on party hats and have noise makers at the ready. The sound of wind is heard.

Nippletitus: Quiet, everyone, someone is arriving.

Mrs. Kowalski: Positions everybody. Alright, one, two, three.

A trendily dressed man appears. He is wearing tap shoes and stops dead in his tracks when he sees the welcoming committee. They blow their noisemakers.

Mrs. Kowalski: Now there's a prince.

Nippletitus: He's good-looking. Not a Zeus, but a well-rounded mortal.

Clyde: I shall converse with the gentleman. I bid you good welcome, sir.

Joey: Oh, hi there.

Clyde: I trust you had a pleasant journey.

Joey: Where am I?

Mrs. Kowalski: Never mind all the crap, Prince. What's your name and where's you from?

Joey: A ... my name is Joey. Who are you guys, anyway? ... Aha, the press!

Clyde: Joey ...?

Joey: I never had a last name. Guess they couldn't think of one. You know writers.

The word "writer" does not sit well with the group. They become agitated.

Clyde: All too well.

Mrs. Kowalski: So where were you cut from Joe?

Joey: Cut?

Nippletitus: Sliced, slashed, dismembered, severed, slit.

Joey: Huh?

Fiddleditch: Ripped, torn, lacerated, chopped.

Mrs. Kowalski: Moved down, lopped off.

Joey: I ... ah ... I don't understand.

Clyde: From which play was your character released?

Joey: Released?

Clyde: Yes, yes, what are you from?

Joey: Oh, a musical.

Clyde: What is the name of the piece?

Joey: It's a new one, perhaps you've heard of it, *HEY DUD!!!?*

Mrs. Kowalski: *Hey Dud?*

Joey: I know it sounds a bit bland, but you really should see it on the marquee with the exclamation marks. *Hey Dud* has three of them. HEY DUD exclamation mark, exclamation mark, exclamation mark. Every good, new musical has to have at least one exclamation mark. It shows excitement and entertainment value!

Nippletitus: What was its revelation to mortal man.

Joey: Huh?

Fiddleditch: She means, what is it about?

Joey: Well, there's been a lot of changes but, basically, it's a sensitive, tender, passionate, but innovative new musical about the love affair between two lovestruck teenagers in the war who inadvertently find an unexploded bomb, and feel compelled to dance with it across the country before it blows up in someone's face.

Fiddleditch: Sounds ... interesting.

Mrs. Kowalski: Sounds stupid.

Joey: Wait till you hear the music, Just fabulous. It's getting better every day. Did I mention the show is going to Broadway? All the way from the regionals. Imagine my character on a Broadway stage!

Clyde: Perhaps it will remain in your imagination.

Joey: What is that supposed to mean? ... Hey who are you guys anyway? I'm supposed to be in re-rehearsal.

Fiddleditch: I don't think he realizes sir.

Mrs. Kowalski: Kinda slow on the uptake if you ask me. Figures— musicals.

Nippletitus: I think he's kinda cute.

Clyde: My good sir, you have no idea why you are here, do you?

Joey: Now I get it, this is some kind of improv game, right? Please, I don't have time to waste here. Things aren't going all that good, rewrites and all that. I really have to get back.

An offstage sob.

Joey: What is this place?

Fiddleditch: It's our home. A rest home. Your home. A home for all the characters that are cut from theatrical productions. Sometimes from the first or second drafts. Or a director doesn't like you. Or because of money. Or …

Mrs. Kowalski: Or maybe you was just a bad idea. Where do you fit in buddy?

Joey: You mean Joey is no longer a character in *Hey Dud!!!*?

Clyde: You have a quick mind.

Joey: But I don't understand. They loved me in Edmonton.

Clyde: Edmonton???

Joey: Everybody loved my character.

Fiddleditch: We were all loved once.

Nippletitus: I think now would be a good time to introduce everyone to Joey.

Clyde: Yes, by all means. Let me present, Nippletitus, late of the Greeks.

Nippletitus: I'm Nippletitus, cut from that great Greek classic, *Oedipus the King*. I was his sister and I was to be his queen. But alas, I have been forsaken. Oh woe, oh woe, oh woe, oh woe, oh woe, oh woe …

Clyde: Oh please, Nippletitus, restrain yourself. And this is Fiddleditch.

Fiddleditch: At your service, sir. I'm trivial, very trivial, but unfortunately I never possessed the wit that true triviality needs in order to survive. So I had the misfortune of being cut, not from one, but from all the plays Oscar Wilde ever wrote. Would you care for a cucumber sandwich?

Joey: Uh ... not right now, thanks.

Clyde: And this ... woman, is Mrs. Kowalski.

Joey: Don't tell me, Stanley's mother.

Mrs. Kowalski: What's it to you?

Joey: You must be very proud of your son.

Mrs. Kowalski: I'd be prouder if I was in the damn play. *Bellowing out like Stanley.* JOEY! JO-EY! What you all looking at, I'm just greeting the new arrival in the Kowalski way.

Joey: Sure. *To Clyde.* And you are?

Clyde: Surely you jest.

Joey: Ah ... no.

Clyde: You mean you don't know?

Joey: I'm afraid not.

Fiddleditch: This is Clyde, Prince of Denmark.

Joey: You're kidding. You mean Hamlet, don't you?

Mrs. Kowalski: Please, don't get him going.

Clyde: No, no, no, no! If you must know, that, that ... Hamlet, he was only a secondary character. The play was about me, me! I had all the lines, until William took them away. Villain, villain, damnéd villain thy name is ... thy name is ... shit!

A loud sob is heard.

Joey: What was that?

Nippletitus: Welcome to your new home.

Fiddleditch: Forever and ever.

Mrs. Kowalski: Amen.

Joey: No, this can't happen. I am well developed. I have strong motivation. An entire sub-plot revolves around me—if not the whole play. My God, I have the key line, "A man without a bomb is nothing."

Clyde: And you mourn for that? What about me, "To be or not to be" or "O what a rogue and peasant slave I am" or "There are more things in heaven and earth … pal … than are dreamt of in your … in your …"

Joey: Philosophy.

Clyde: I know my lines.

Mrs. Kowalski: If they're your lines, how come you keep getting them wrong?

Clyde: I do not, I do not. I just have a lot to remember.

Mrs. Kowalski: Bull. That's why you're here, your character couldn't cut it.

Clyde: Why don't you go soak your head.

Mrs. Kowalski: My, my, Prince, the ol' blank verse sure has gone downhill.

Another sob is heard.

Fiddleditch: Please. We must decide to which wing Joey should go.

Mrs. Kowalski: Put him in the Shaw Wing.

Fiddleditch: Oh no, you don't want to go the George Bernard Shaw Wing, those characters never stop talking. You'd never get any sleep. I think there's room in the Absurdist Wing.

Mrs. Kowalski: I wouldn't wish my worst enemy there, those guys are crazy in the head.

Clyde: How about the Samuel French Annex, there's always room for one more there.

Everyone giggles.

Nippletitus: No, we couldn't do that. Even the gods would not do such a thing … You could stay with me if you like.

Joey: Yeah … tight … sure.

Clyde: No need. We will find him suitable lodgings.

Mrs. Kowalski: How about him bunking with you, Prince? You got a whole wing to yourself.

Joey: A whole wing. You mean …

Mrs. Kowalski: That's right, Clyde here is the only character ol' Willy Shakespeare ever cut. He must have thought of the prince here on a really bad day.

Clyde: Perhaps. But doesn't it make your blood boil to know that you were replaced by that madwoman Blanche DuBois.

Mrs. Kowalski: Who told you that? It's not true. Who's the bastard who told you that? You Brits think you know everything.

Clyde: I am not British, I'm a Dane.

Mrs. Kowalski: A Dane? I thought that was a dog. Blanche just fit the part better. No one would have believed that Stanley would treat his mama like that. I don't care what anybody says, Stanley was a good boy.

Fiddleditch: Please stop. Now why don't we all pause, and … and … have a refreshing cucumber sandwich.

All: NO!

Another loud sob.

Joey: Who is that anyway, and why is he always crying? *Nippletitus whispers in his ear.* Makes sense….

Nippletitus: Let us go, Joey.

Clyde: Remember, Nippletitus, our meeting tonight.

Nippletitus: Perhaps not tonight Prince, I think you would have trouble understanding Greek. … You know Joey, Oedipus didn't know what he was missing. I mean I am a very affectionate and loving character. And I have no guilt feelings about anything because I know everything is out of our hands. It is all up to the gods to decide. Do you understand what I am saying?

Joey: Well … no.

Nippletitus: Well it's like you being cut and me being cut. And both of us being here—now—at the same time. It's fate. There's nothing you can do about it except let it happen. Now do you understand?

Joey: Yeah, sure, right. Okay.

Nippletitus: You have nice eyes, Joey. Oedipus had nice eyes. But let's not get into that right now.

They walk offstage together.

Clyde: A vile, vile, ungodly man.

Mrs. Kowalski: What is it now?

Clyde: I do not care for the peasant.

Fiddleditch: He seems perfectly nice to me. I like nice.

Clyde: He is a modern. A base and illegitimate modern who sucks the life life and vigour from the real theatre.

Mrs. Kowalski: Hey, you just watch who you're talking to, buddy, I'm not that old myself.

Fiddleditch: May I interject to say that there is modern—and then there is modern. Wouldn't you say that is correct, sir?

Clyde: *Musing.* Perhaps.

Mrs. Kowalski: Cut the whole "perhaps" crap, say what you mean or shut up. That's the whole problem with you people, you never say what you mean. It gives me a headache.

Clyde: Then perhaps you should not *sit* so long, my dear lady.

Mrs. Kowalski: You're a real gem, aren't you. A character among characters, a real prince. But I know what you really are, a real princess!

Clyde: You're so uncouth.

Mrs. Kowalski: You're such an asshole.

Fiddleditch: A-hem. Would anybody care for a cucumber sandwich before I leave?

Clyde and Mrs. Kowalski: NO!

Sob offstage. Fiddleditch hurries off like a frightened rabbit. Clyde and Mrs. Kowalski are silent for a moment.

Mrs. Kowalski: You know, you wouldn't be such a bad character if you didn't have your nose so goddamned high in the air.

Clyde: Really.

Mrs. Kowalski: And for what? Just because you're a Shakespearean character. Big deal, I'm sorry, maybe you can fool other people with all that highbrow stuff, but with me it don't wash. Dressing all in black—who you trying to impress anyway. You better get it through your thick *skull* that you ain't better than anybody else. You're cut just like the rest of us.

Clyde: *Taking hold of Mrs. Kowalski's head.* A skull, yes, a skull … in my hands … "Alas poor Yorick. I knew him. A fellow of infinite … of infinite …"

Mrs. Kowalski: Stomach.

Clyde: No.

Mrs. Kowalski: Feet?

Clyde: No, no, that is not it. Why is it I cannot remember? Why? Why? Oh my curséd soul.

Mrs. Kowalski: Okay, all right. I didn't mean anything by what I said. I'm like that. Take it easy, you really got to get a grip on yourself.

Clyde: How can I ever go back if I cannot remember? I would be a wondrous good character. I could suffer all the slings and a bunch of arrows of outrageous … something … for another chance.

Mrs. Kowalski: I know, I know, you don't have to tell me about it. You know I coulda been a character, but now I'm just a cut, which is what I am. … Playwrights! They think they're so high and mighty, but you know what they really are? Pricks with a pen. Especially the ones that go around with the three names, two of them ain't good enough. La-di-da.

Clyde: How true. *Pause. He unsheathes his sword.* Death to all writers!

Mrs. Kowalski: You betcha!

A loud sob is heard. Fiddleditch hurries on stage still carrying his plate of sandwiches. He is also carrying a piece of paper.

Fiddleditch: Excuse me. *Moving closer slowly.* Excuse me … excuse me.

Clyde: I have told you, Fiddleditch, time and time again, I do not want a cucumber sandwich.

Fiddleditch: It's not that, sir. A message has just come concerning the new arrival.

Mrs. Kowalski: I'll take it.

Clyde: I'll take it.

Mrs. Kowalski: Ah, give it to him, it makes him feel important.

Clyde: *Taking the paper and reading aloud.* This is to inform you that the character Joey, who had been cut from the new innovative musical, *HEY DUD!!!* has been reinstated to perform his duties as plot motivator during the upcoming Broadway run. Please inform the character Joey of the above changes immediately. Thank you. Sincerely, the Top.

Mrs. Kowalski: What the hell does that mean?

Fiddleditch: It means that Joey isn't cut after all.

Clyde: God's bodkins, man. When a person is cut, it is final. That is to say a person can not be uncut.

Mrs. Kowalski: What's all the fuss, Prince, let him go. Aw, I say let him go, who needs another of them guys around here anyway?

Clyde: You forget, dear lady, that if Joey returns to *Dud*, he will have a tale to tell, and I'm afraid that we, as characters, will not fare well.

Fiddleditch: Oh dear, dear.

Mrs. Kowalski: Listen, let the jerk go, I didn't have much use for him either but at least one of us is getting a second chance.

Clyde: Another chance? *Daydreaming.* Another chance ...

Mrs. Kowalski: Aw, I've had enough. I'm going to the bar, maybe if I'm lucky I'll meet one of those Off-Broadway pansies and terrorize the hell out of 'im. Wanna come?

Fiddleditch: I'm not sure I want to see that. I have such a gentle disposition.

Mrs. Kowalski: Sure, c'mon, it'll be good for you. You gonna come, Prince? Should be good for a few laughs. God knows you could use some.

Clyde: Perhaps not. Anon, anon.

Mrs. Kowalski: Suit yourself Prince. C'mon Fiddleditch, if you play your cards right, you can buy me a drink.

Fiddleditch: But sir, what about the message?

Clyde: Fear not, Fiddleditch, the message will be delivered.

Mrs. Kowalski and Fiddleditch exit. Clyde stands alone, deep in thought.

Clyde: To be a character or not to be a character, that is the question. If the character is the thing, is it not better that the character be seen. Whether 'tis nobler to suffer the slings and arrows of outrageous production or not to strut the stage at all. Methinks the former will suffice. If this *Hey Dud!!!* be liken to a dog, I shall be a flea on its ear, rather than live a wasted existence here. Here then is my plan, I will no longer be all in black and have spirits lowly, I will be full of pomp and very showy. And soon I will be on the boards once more, no longer as Clyde, but as Joey.

Nippletitus and Joey return. They are arm in arm.

Clyde: Greetings. I trust the tour is complete.

Joey: Hiya Prince. You know this isn't such a bad place. Don't get me wrong, I don't really dig the idea of being cut, but if a guy has to be cut, this isn't a bad place, especially if you have a lovely lady like Nipple here, to show you around. *Nippletitus giggles.* Only thing is, you should spruce up your lobby a little, maybe get some plants. A waterfall would be nice.

Clyde: Indeed. *He hides the letter.*

Nippletitus: You should hear the story Joey has to tell of a shameless man, a spineless man, a senseless man …

Joey: … the general manager. He said there wasn't enough money to pay for all the cast, so I was cut. I'm sure of it. You can't trust anybody.

Nippletitus: Isn't that the most terrible thing you ever heard?

Clyde: Yes, a crime most foul. My dear Nippletitus, I wonder if you might take your leave so Joey and I might have a chance to converse alone, character to character.

Nippletitus: No, we have pressing needs to attend to.

Clyde: Please, dear Nippletitus, a minute, then I shall leave you two completely alone … forever.

Nippletitus: All right, but don't be long Joey, I want to show you how developed my character really is.

Joey: Yes, yes, right away.

Nippletitus exits.

Joey: Hey Prince, whatever you got to say could you make it quick. Nippletitus there is pretty hot stuff and I'd like to get back to her before she starts to cool down. … So, what's up?

Clyde: I would like very much to learn more about you.

Joey: You want to find out more about me?

Clyde: Yes, I find you of infinite fascination and wonder.

Joey: You do?! My, that is quite a compliment, and coming from a man of your stature. I'm honoured.

Clyde: It is the artist in me that allows me to speak of such things.

Joey: I am flattered. But I think you're just putting me on. Characters like you are always thumbing their noses at characters like me.

Clyde: Nothing could ever be farther from the light of truth. What I speak, I speak in total earnest; completely free of the shackles of deceit.

Joey: No foolin'?

Clyde: No foolin'. It is because of where you stand in the spectrum of the theatre. You are at its cutting edge. You are to be admired humbly by those such as I, whose day has come and gone and whose night is now endless.

Joey: Wow! I never thought of it that way.

Clyde: Indeed, you are a god, compared to lowly characters such as we.

Joey: A god. I like that. I like that a lot. That certainly should impress Nippletitus.

Clyde: It certainly should. Now Joey, I wonder if you maybe could confide to me the fine craft of your characterization.

Joey: My characterization?

Clyde: Yes, what it is that makes you tick, as it were.

Joey: Well, I dream of being a character in a hit production on Broadway.

Clyde: Yes, yes, I realize that, but what I am talking about is your motivation within the play.

Joey: Oh that. My motivation is to defuse the bomb, when the two lovestruck teenagers deliver it to me.

Clyde: Is that all?

Joey: *Defensively.* Well it's a large cast, and we all can't be stars, now can we?

Clyde: Of course not. A play is a sum of its characters, no matter how small. Now, by you defusing said bomb, you do, in fact, bring about the resolution to the plot?

Joey: Well I thought that was what I was supposed to do, but now that I'm here, I don't know how they're going to end it. Maybe they're gonna let it blow up and make a statement. Everyone wants to make a statement nowadays. All I want is to make it on Broadway.

Clyde: A sad state of affairs to be sure.

Joey: I even had a song. A solo at that.

Clyde: A song?

Joey: Yes. "Bomb of Love."

Clyde: Sounds … musical. Would you might teach me?

Joey: You want to learn my song?

Clyde: Yes, by all means. If you feel I am worthy. After all, it's god's music.

Joey: Yeah, well I guess it is, but right now?

Clyde: Oh, if it please you m'lord. Shall we begin?

Joey: Sure, why not. It's uptempo. A nice beat with catchy lyrics. Now repeat after me.

Joey and Clyde: *A song and dance routine.*

> A man without a bomb is nothing
> But if it blows, he's less
> Detonation's always painful;
> Not to mention the mess.

Clyde: Perhaps, Joey, the task before me would be made easier if I donned part of your garb. For the sake of the character.

Joey: Yeah, sure, of course. For the sake of the character.

Joey takes his jacket off and gives it to Clyde. It is not a perfect fit. They go through the song again.

Joey: Alright the second verse is just like the first but the words are different and the music changes.

Clyde: *Looks at Joey, puzzled for a moment, but goes along with it.* Got it.

Clyde and Joey: *Singing and dancing:*

> But for the sake of love, darling,
> I will forget the risk.
> This bomb is our love's salvation,
> Set off with a kiss.
> *Chorus.*
> So bombard me with love, baby.
> Explode my load.
> Kingdom come me, honey.
> Make me hard to hold.

Clyde: Methinks this is most enjoyable.

Joey: You do?! Wow! Boy, if you like it, I wonder why in the world I was cut.

Clyde: There are more things in heaven and earth, Joe, than are dreamt of in your theatre.

Joey: Prince?

Clyde: What is it?

Joey: I was wondering if you could show me some of your stuff, you know, if you don't mind. A character like me doesn't get much of a chance to do, well, you know.

Clyde: Yes, yes, of course, I will teach you forthright the fine aspect of my art. It will be my pleasure.

Joey: Hey, alright.

Clyde: First, fix in your imagination this, the stage, the realm of your being. Now, go to, explore it's boundaries, and once you find the edge of your universe, and stand bravely erec ... *Exasperated.* Go to the edge of the stage and stand there, all right? *Joey goes to the edge of the stage.* Now do not turn around, or the magic is broken.

Joey: All right Prince. Now what? What's my line?

Clyde: Oh no don't speak, not yet, just stand there exuding intensity, power and moodiness.

Joey: Like this?

Clyde: No, something is missing. Oh, give me your shoes.

Joey: My shoes? I don't know ...

Clyde: I'll give you my sword.

Joey: Oh, okay. Deal.

They make the exchange. Clyde is preparing himself for his exit.

Clyde: Fine, fine, now you are exuding wondrously well.

Joey: Why thank you, that is very nice of you to say so. Geez, you're a really sweet guy after all. Now what's my line?

Clyde: *Slowly.* Good-bye, sour sight, parting is such sweet delight.

Joey: Good-bye, sour sight, parting is such sweet delight.

Clyde: *Faster.* I will walk no more on this barren shore, for I am back on stage tonight.

Clyde exits.

Joey: What? What's that you say? What's on the barren shore? What's next? Anything? C'mon, I taught you my song. I gave you my shoes. Prince? Prince Clyde of Denmark? Are you there? *Turning around.* Clyde, where are you? Clyde? Clyde? CLYDE!

A really loud sob is heard.

Blackout.

Scene Two

The same place, later. Mrs. Kowalski and Fiddleditch are on stage. Mrs. Kowalski is seated and Fiddleditch is scratching her back.

Mrs. Kowalski: Well, what do you say Fiddleditch? It's just like that Elizabethan windbag to pull a stunt like this.

Fiddleditch: This has all the markings of quite a scandal, quite a scandal indeed. Something like this has never happened before, it looks very bad, very bad indeed.

Mrs. Kowalski: Yeah, and it's all the fault of the prince. I wouldn't care if the melancholy jerk never came back, but a character can't be a character other than himself. He knows that.

Fiddleditch: How true, it goes against all the rules of nature, and proper decorum and manners.

Mrs. Kowalski: Yeah, sure, but you gotta hand it to him, I never thought he had it in him to do something like this. He must have been really desperate, I mean Clyde, the prince of Denmark in *HEY DUD!!!* Kinda boggles the mind, don't it. ... Hey Fiddleditch, how 'bout a little down and to the left, ohhhh … yeah, you got nice hands Fiddleditch.

Fiddleditch: It comes from cutting all those cucumbers.

Mrs. Kowalski: You're a very weird character, Fiddleditch, but you're okay.

Fiddleditch: Thank you. That is very kind of you to say so.

Mrs. Kowalski: *Goes into a Blanche DuBois persona.* I knew a person once with hands like yours ... he was a boy, just a boy, when I was a very young girl. When I was sixteen, I made the discovery—love. *Fiddleditch giggles. If looks could kill he'd be dead.* Aw, I guess I would laugh too, to hear myself. I coulda never got away with saying those lines anyway. "I've always depended on the kindness of strangers." What kind of character says those things. Huh! I've never depended on anything—let alone kindness.

Fiddleditch: I'm a kind character, if you don't mind my saying so, I'm just not funny.

Nippletitus enters.

Mrs. Kowalski: Any luck?

Nippletitus: I seek, but cannot find Joey anywhere.

Fiddleditch: He did take the news very badly.

Mrs. Kowalski: I sorta feel for the guy, you know. I guess it's not his fault he's such a chump. But I tell ya, we're not going to look too good, we were supposed to make him feel welcome and this happens. You know, Fiddleditch, it's all your fault. You should have never given the message to Clyde.

Fiddleditch: Me? If you hadn't dragged me off to that bar ...

Mrs. Kowalski: Well, nobody twisted your arm ...

Fiddleditch: Madam, you would have broken it if I had refused.

Nippletitus: Please! We have all failed in our duties. If we ever find him, we must have a festival in his honour.

Mrs. Kowalski: A party!? You think that's going to cheer him up? Can't wait till he meets the boys from the morality plays. Great bunch of partiers. Laugh a decade.

Nippletitus: Well, we should do something, to be cut is one thing, but to be uncut, and still be here, is quite another.

Fiddleditch: Perhaps his was the unkindest cut of all. … My, that was witty. Wasn't that witty? Wasn't it?

Mrs. Kowalski: You're a scream, Fiddleditch, just a scream.

A sob is heard. Joey enters whistling.

Joey: Hi, guys, how's it going?

Nippletitus: Joey!

Fiddleditch: How are you, Joey?

Joey: Oh, all right.

Nippletitus: You know, Joey, the gods will avenge the wrong done to you.

Joey: That's nice.

Mrs. Kowalski: Now listen Joe, I'm the first to say that what Clyde did to you was pretty sleazy, but you're going to have to get used to it.

Joey: All right.

Fiddleditch: I assure you we will give you all the support you need.

Joey: Appreciate it.

Nippletitus: You don't have to face this alone.

Joey: Suppose not.

Mrs. Kowalski: You just have to learn to fill the time. You could do like me, you could go to the bar. 'Course that gets downright dull after awhile but, hey, it's something to do.

Joey: Sounds real fun.

Nippletitus: Or you could recite epic poems as I do, for days, weeks at a time. You'd be surprised at how fast the centuries fly by once you get the rhythm.

Joey: Oh boy.

Fiddleditch: Or you could do something really exciting: cucumber cutting. It is quite an art, but I feel that you have the right temperament to make a first-rate cucumber cutter. We will begin with the basics immediately, there is no reason for delay.

Joey: Whoa, hold on there! Look, I appreciate what you people are trying to do, but you're just wasting your time. I've done a lot of thinking and this place won't be so bad for a few hours, until they find out ol' Clyde is the wrong character and, the way he dances, it's just a matter of time 'til they do. In the meantime, it's best for you all to remember that I'm not like you people. I'm not a … I never was a …

Mrs. Kowalski: Never was a what?

Joey: Oh, never mind.

Fiddleditch: Never mind what?

Joey: It's nothing really.

Fiddleditch: I, for one, would like to know what I am that you're not.

Nippletitus: Me too, Joey.

Joey: Well, all I wanted to say was, in a simple sort of way, that because … see, it's like this, I wasn't really cut, and because I came here on false pretenses, I'm not really like you all, I'm not a …

Mrs. Kowalski: Say it loud and clear.

Joey: It's just that I'm not … it's just that I'm not a … loser.

Sob.

Mrs. Kowalski: What?

Joey: *Pause, then defiantly.* I'm not a loser; I'm not an unacceptable characterization.

Mrs. Kowalski: Where the hell do you come off calling us unacceptable characterizations you little …

Nippletitus: Wait, I don't think he meant it that way. You didn't mean it that way did you Joey?

Joey: Yeah … sure I did.

Pause. Another sob.

Fiddleditch: I say, I feel ill.

Nippletitus: Oh cruel, cruel. I have been forsaken, oh woe, oh woe, I have been forsaken, oh woe.

Joey: Hey, hey, hey, guys, lighten-up. I'm sorry you feel that way but that's how it is. Look, you're all grown up characters, you understand that characters that are cut don't hold a candle to legitimate characters, like me. That's life, show biz … Look, I shouldn't be here, I'm real, but as long as I am here, you guys have to face facts. I've thought about this, and I've come to the conclusion that … I'm superior. Yeah, that's it. I'm a god compared to you … a very warm god.

Nippletitus: Blasphemer. Blasphemer. Blasphemer.

Joey: I didn't really want to get into this right now, but I'm glad that we got all the cards on the table. No hard feelings, all right? *Joey wipes his brow.*

Joey: Hey Fiddleditch, you think you could get me something to eat—no cucumber sandwiches, all right? Some real food, something to sink your teeth into. How 'bout you Kowalski? I bet you could whip up a helluva meal, feeding that boy of yours. Why don't you just wander to the kitchen and see what you can come up with. And some water, lots of water with lots of ice. Nippletitus can go give you a hand, all right girls?

Another sob.

Joey: And on your way there, would one of you want to something about that, put a gag on him or something. He's beginning to give me a headache … Well, move it.

Nobody moves.

Joey: Look, I didn't want to do this, but you leave me no choice. Fiddleditch, come here. *Fiddleditch moves cautiously to Joey.* Be funny. Make me laugh. *Silence.* Whatsa matter Fiddleditch? Isn't that what your character is supposed to be, witty? Your funny bone got a crack in it? Thought so. And you Nippletitus, are you going to spend a nice romantic evening with ol' Oedipussy tonight? Guess not. Guess with him every day is mother's day. Now Fiddleditch, that's funny.

Joey: And Mrs. Kowalski, so sensitive, so fragile, gentle as a rose ... petal—what do you say Mrs. K? You think you fit the bill? Didn't think so—geez, I'm burning up—you see, I'm the new order, the cutting edge of dramatic expression. You all had your chance and you blew it.

Mrs. Kowalski: This boy is looking for a major re-rewrite.

Nippletitus: You two start with his motivation, I'll go for his subtext.

Mrs. Kowalski: One, two, three! Let's get him.

The two attack Joey. They grab him on either side, but soon realize that they do not know what to do with him.

Joey: Please don't hurt me.

Mrs. Kowalski: Don't just sit there, Fiddleditch, do something.

Fiddleditch: I don't know what to do, sir ... ah ... madam.

Joey: Please, it was Clyde that said I was a god, really, maybe I'm just a little superior.

Nippletitus: By Zeus, do something!

Fiddleditch takes out an English cucumber, and bops Joey on the head. Joey lets out a scream and drops to the floor.

Nippletitus: You killed him.

Fiddleditch: With a cucumber?

Mrs. Kowalski: Well he ain't moving. *She kicks him.* Looks dead. I didn't think it could happen. I knew, Fiddleditch, those cucumbers would be good for something.

Fiddleditch: *Inspecting the weapon.* An English cucumber, no less.

As they all look at Joey's lifeless body, Clyde hurries on stage. He looks a little worse for the wear. He is shoeless, dirty, and his face is covered in soot. He is upstage of the group.

Clyde: Goodnight, sweet Joey, a character with such tough luck does not even have the fortune to be cut. Indeed, he is dead.

Nippletitus: Clyde!

Mrs. Kowalski: I don't believe it, he's back.

Fiddleditch: It is so good to see you, sir. So much has happened in your absence. I killed Joey with a cucumber.

Clyde: Fear not, Fiddleditch, the weapon of Joey's miscontent is not in your hand, it was a fire that burnt out of his mortal coil.

Fiddleditch: A fire, sir?

Clyde: I will explain, anon, anon. The playwright, the architect of that dud musical, is a madman. He is a lost soul in a theatrical maze. After agonizing over a script that should be ripped, he set fire to all copies, all drafts, all notes, he even burned down the theatre and promptly lost his mind. The musical *Hey Dud!!!* Has vanished forever, leaving not even a cut character to mourn its passing.

Mrs. Kowalski: But what about you, you were in the play, how come you didn't get torched?

Clyde: My escape from the flames was narrow. My salvation was that my originality was that of Shakespeare, not of that other madman. The Bard saved my cut soul. I rejoice in that fact. Oh William, I curse you not ever again.

Mrs. Kowalski: Cut the poetics and tell us what it was like.

Fiddleditch: Yes, please tell us.

Clyde: It was a horrendous experience. Methinks there is something rotten in the state of ... the theatre.

Fiddleditch: I say, as bad as that sir?

Clyde: A nightmare. Concepts, contracts, production, profits. My God, the play was cast according to whom fit the costumes. Right down to the director and musicians.

Nippletitus: The horror, the horror.

Clyde: It left a bad taste that all the water of the oceans could not wash out.

Mrs. Kowalski: I coulda told you that. *Pause.* So you're back.

Clyde: Yes, dear lady, I am. Slightly the worse for wear. *He takes his sword from Joey.* But still in character.

Nippletitus: Well, I do hope you learned your lesson.

Clyde: It was a bitter education.

Mrs. Kowalski: But, what the heck, you got to go back on stage for a little while, no matter how bad it was, you still got to strut your stuff. You know that was pretty fast thinking to take Joey's place like that.

Clyde: Yes, that is my curse.

Fiddleditch: Your curse, sir?

Clyde: I've always had a nimble mind. I have always been able to make fast decisions, and alas, that is my downfall. I always knew what had to be done, and did it, unlike my brother. So when it was *CLYDE Prince of Denmark* it was a one-act.

Mrs. Kowalski: That's why you were cut.

Clyde: Yes, it is my lot. Adieu, adieu, adieu. Sweet, sweet fame and fortune. I knew you well once. But alas, I am too condemned to the dark and dreadful abyss of well-intentioned but poorly-conceived paintings of the mind. I am nothing but a brush stroke gone mad; easily erased and quickly forgotten. So here we are, here to live among our memories, not as sweet as those that might have been. The sun that had risen with such promise has been untimely snuffed out before it produced its glorious noon-day light. And here we are, to wallow in the darkest recesses of labour lost that once had the brightest potential.

Pause. They all sit quietly. Then …

Nippletitus: I was wondering, Fiddleditch, if you knew any Greek.

Fiddleditch: No, but I always wanted to. Unfortunately, I'm such a slow study.

Nippletitus: Why don't you come to my place, I could give you a few lessons.

Fiddleditch: I'd like that, but do you really think I could learn?

Nippletitus: I don't know. We could try.

Fiddleditch: Shall I bring me English cucumber?

Nippletitus: Please do.

Nippletitus and Fiddleditch exit.

Mrs. Kowalski: You know Prince, that wasn't such a bad speech, a little long-winded, as usual, but not bad. And when you really think about it, this isn't such a bad place.

Clyde: After my leap across the spectrum, methinks not.

Mrs. Kowalski: Well, all I can see is that you're looking pretty burnt-out, Prince. What do say about coming to my place and I'll fix you a meal like I used to do for my boy, Stanley.

Clyde: Well …

Mrs. Kowalski: I thought you was such a fast-thinker, come on, I only offer once.

Clyde: Your offer sounds … delightful Mrs. Kowalski.

Mrs. Kowalski: You know you do remind me of my boy a bit. *Bellowing.* CLYDE! CLYDE! But it sure don't have the same ring, does it. C'mon, let's go.

Clyde: You have solicited, Mrs. Kowalski … the rest is silence.

She grabs him by the arm and yanks him away. They exit. The stage is empty. A few moments later an old man shuffles on stage. He is dressed in old baggy pajamas. He is sniffling and sobbing softly. It is evident that he has been the person crying throughout the play. He seems lost and looks around. When his back is turned, the name GODOT can clearly be seen embroidered on the back of his pajama top. He spies the sandwiches and goes to them. He picks one up and takes a bite. He chews slowly and swallows. He then looks straight at the audience.

Godot: Where is everybody?

He shrugs, continues eating.

Blackout.

Lyle Victor Albert in *Scraping the Surface.*
Photo by The Edmonton Journal.

Scraping
the Surface

Scraping the Surface was first produced in a one-act version at Vancouver's Men's Fest in August 1995, with Richard Lett as director. The two-act version premiered at Theatre Network in Edmonton in March 1996, with Ron Jenkins as director. It was produced by Fringe Theatre Adventures and Theatre Network, and received the Elizabeth Sterling Hayes award for Outstanding New Play of the 1996/96 season. A version of *Scraping the Surface* for young audiences was produced in Vancouver by Theatre Terrific, directed by Jamie Norris. That version won Vancouver's Jessie Richardson Award in 1997 for script and performance by an actor for high schools.

ACT ONE

Lights up on Vic, centre stage in front of a table covered with a towel.

Vic: In the age of uncertainty, disillusionment, disappointment, disaffection, self-doubt and boredom, there are always those who will embark on heroic pursuits in order to feel alive ... Some bungy jump, some race automobiles, some leap from planes ... I *pulls away towel, exposing a basin with assorted shaving equipment* ... Shave.

With a razor and a can of cream, I push the envelope of my existence ... three times a week.

You might laugh, you might scoff, you might say, "So what? I do it too." But the fact remains that when I put sharp metal to soft skin, there is a leap of faith wider than you will ever know. It's true. Anything can happen. The phone could ring. An ambulance could wail past my apartment. A dog might suddenly begin to howl ... all these things can lead to instant disaster because I am referred to by the medical community and also by people who know what they are talking about as ... JUMPY.

And I'm grateful for that because, for me, shaving is not just a function of good personal grooming. For me, it's an adventure. It's a little like golf: you have fairways, you have roughs, you have a short game, bunkers and, of course, you have water. And although I know the course intimately, I never know how I'm going to play it day to day. The best you can do is pick up a club ... and hope you don't slice.

But like anything worthwhile, a good clean shave doesn't just happen. There are bumps and turns and detours and sweat and tears and a little blood. But I can tell you this: it's been worth it, because there was once a time when all of this might never have happened.

December 23, 1977. I had just turned seventeen and for the first time in my life I needed a shave. Not that you could tell, mind you. At ten paces, all you might see was a boyish grin and freckles. But I knew in my heart when I looked in the mirror: they were coming.

And I was right: fifty or so facial follicles had rallied together and decided to make an appearance. I figured my body was giving me a birthday present. I was overjoyed ... but being a North American male of European descent, another instinct quickly took over. Because they were there, I had to cut 'em down.

My parents must have sensed this because on the day of my birthday I was presented with a box all neatly wrapped with ribbons and bows and a card that read, "We know you could really use this now...."

It's an innocent enough statement, but whenever I heard it, little bells went off inside my head. It meant I was getting something that was good for me. Which is great. Everybody needs something that's good for them. But let me ask you this: when you're eight years old and jumpy ... and your sister gives you a Meccano set for Christmas, is that really good for you? I mean, here you have tiny, tiny nuts and tiny, tiny bolts, and the idea is to attach the tiny, tiny nuts to the tiny, tiny bolts. Then you take a little, little screwdriver and a little, little wrench and you try to tighten the tiny, tiny nuts to the tiny, tiny bolts. And when you've done this 10,204 times, you have something big. Which you have to take apart because it's time to go to bed—or in my case, time to go to university.

The theory behind giving me the Meccano set was that it would teach me patience, concentration and co-ordination. And God knows those are three things I really can use. But when my other sister gave me the "Operation" game, *buzzer sound effect*, you lose. I began to suspect that maybe my family had a different agenda. Oh, sure, they loved me, but in the days before cable, I was the best entertainment around.

But a present is a present, no matter what dark forces motivate the giver. Here was mine. I quickly unwrapped it, opened the box and there it was ... a Remington Mach III, XL 2000 Special Edition. To call this just an electric shaver would be like calling a Lamborghini good transportation or the Mona Lisa a nice painting. NO, this went far beyond electric shaver. This was art: four independent rotary heads of thousands of titanium-tipped blades which all float on a silicon solution. Its five-speed, air-cooled electric motor was encased in a jet-black chassis made from the latest space-age polymers. Indeed, astronauts had died in the development of this perfect shaving instrument. I picked it up and held it in my hand, instantly feeling the power and the awe of millions of years of human evolution and innovation coursing through my veins. What a rush. Then my mother spoke in her usual pragmatic mother's voice. "You better not break it, dear. It cost us a bundle."

Of course I would shave, but not in the dingy confines of a bathroom, with only a mirror to reflect this momentous event. No, I wanted to share my first cutting. My first flirtation with manhood—I wanted to share it with the universe. So I clutched my Remington Mach III XL 2000 Special Edition and ran outside. Why? Because I could. It was cordless!

I stood out in the middle of the yard, the shaver welded to my fist like something out of Terminator. It was part of me and I was part of it, so when I finally managed to turn it on, I was suddenly seduced by its monotonous melody.

Razor sound.

I raised it to my cheek with the same glorious promise as a lover's first kiss. It was unbelievable: silky smooth as it glided effortlessly over my facial features; tenderly caressing as it removed any and all signs of virgin growth. I looked towards the heavens and said, "Yes, this is the best a man can get." And as I looked up, I saw clouds whirling together, weaving together in tighter and tighter and tighter concentric formations. The wind picked up and then … boom! A thunder clap sounded, charging the air with supersonic energy … and being Jumpy, I jumped!

The shaver flew out of my hand and ascended skywards. It made a graceful arc and just as it began its descent towards earth, a lightning bolt shot out, striking it, instantly dissolving it into liquid … Wow … which then rained little electronic teardrops down upon my cleanly shaven face.

My Remington Mach III XL 2000 Special Edition was gone. Vanished. Dissolved into another cosmic reality. It didn't matter because all I had time for was to ponder one single ramification: how was I going to explain this to Mom and Dad?

For the record, and I'm sure you'll appreciate this because it means you're not alone, my parents didn't buy a single word of that story.

So now it's my prickly duty to tell you what really happened. Back in the late sixties, three men from the Lone Star State of Texas got together and decided not to shave. Their names are Billy Gibbons, Dusty Hill and Frank Beard. Collectively, they are known as Z (Zee) Z(Zee) Top, or, in Canadian, Zed Zed Top. And I gotta tell ya, this power trio warmed my rock 'n' roll soul like a southern wind blowin' off the mighty Rio Grande … I was a FAN.

But I was a fan with no money, so when the guys decided to make a pilgrimage to the frozen north and play just for me, I was in a bit of a quandary. ZZ Top—No Money. ZZ Top—No Money. ZZ Top—No Money. ZZ Top—Shaver!

In a flash I went to the bookshelf and pulled out the only truly well-read book in Canada—The Simpson-Sears Catalogue. Shavers, shavers. AHA, Shavers. A Remington Mach III XL 2000 Special Edition … $54.95. ZZ Top tickets cost, on the floor, $13.25. I had a plan.

Now, you ever try to sell a shaver? Even an exceptional one? It's not easy. It's like trying to sell your underwear. Everybody's got at least one, and they don't want yours ... at any price.

Finally, I unloaded it for seventeen bucks to this weird guy I knew, Lenny. Lenny also had a plan. He was going to take the shaver, strip off all the electronics and build ... a bomb. Which he would use to blow up the biggest grain elevator in Alberta. Which would then get his picture on the cover of *Alberta Report*. Which would then be a natural stepping stone into Alberta politics—a very weird guy, Lenny. But it worked. He's now Ralph Klein's bodyguard, and he's a very busy, busy guy....

But that's not important. What's important is that I sold the shaver, I bought the tickets, I went to the concert and did the usual concert stuff.

ZZ Top music, Vic dances, tokes and drinks, lighting a lighter.

Rock ON! ...Then it was over.

I'm skipping over the concert really quickly because it's been my experience that the really dumb, the really stupid, the really asinine things you do in order to get what you want ... those things stick with you longer than the thing you wanted to do in the first place.

It was about a week later when I began to feel the inherent problem with my plan. My mom picked up on it immediately: "We paid good money for that shaver, now shave!"

"Okay, Mom, no problem, any minute now."

After two days of trying to hold her at bay, I knew I had two options: I could either tell the truth ... or take matters into my own hands. Either way, there was going to be blood.

So with the remaining money from my brilliant sale, I went to the drugstore.

"Gimme a Bic razor, and a can of shaving cream ... and you better throw in some of those Bandaids.

And then I went home. I immediately went into the bathroom, laid my purchases in front of me and stared at them … for a long time. I figured it might be a good idea to do some warmups.

Vic does finger warmups and the sign of the cross.

And so I began.

Takes a balloon and blows it up.

I learned this trick from an old National Film Board documentary I saw years ago. It was called "Barbers on the Prairies: Not a Love Story." What I gleaned from this doc is that if you could shave a balloon, you could shave anything.

And the great thing about a balloon is that its movements at times closely resemble my own. But let me assure you that the term airhead has never been applied to me.

Oh, yeah, this was going to be easier than I thought. And I held on to the promise that if I could shave this, *pointing to balloon*, I could shave this, *pointing to face*!

But every time you think you've got it all figured out, you've probably forgotten something essential to your well-being, like your mother. She burst through the door, took one look at me and stopped dead in her tracks. There I was, a can of shaving cream in one hand, a balloon in the other.

Mom didn't say much. In fact, for the first few seconds she said nothing at all. She just looked at me like she was looking at one of those 3D-calendars, trying to find some meaning, some recognizable image, through all the chaos. And when she finally did speak, she said the four most devastating words I had ever heard coming from her mouth: "It's time for supper."

I think you know what I'm talking about. It's that secret weapon that parents have, which they seldom use, but when they do, it totally messes up their kids. It's called not acting like they are supposed to.

I was expecting, "What in Sam Hell are you doing?" or, "Have you completely lost your mind?" or at the very least, a little cuff behind the ear. But NOOOOOO. All I got was, "It's time for supper." Man, that's cold.

By the time dessert arrived, I was ready to confess to anything. Because I knew they knew and the reason they weren't saying anything was because they were going to ambush me when I least expected it.

I didn't sleep for two days. So on the third day, at the breakfast table, when my father looked me in the eye and said, "Pass the sugar," I lost it.

"OK, OK, OK, I sold my shaver so I could go to a ZZ Top concert and I bought a Bic razor so I could shave so you wouldn't notice and that's why I was shaving a balloon because I needed the practice before I did myself because I knew you would be really mad if I got blood on the bathroom floor. OK. You satisfied now? Why don't you just kill me!!!

It was then that my father offered up one of his great non-sequiturs. "You'll be graduating soon ... won't you?

Fact is, he was right. I would be graduating in the spring, but I didn't have a clue what I would be doing afterwards. I think my father secretly hoped that whatever it was, I'd be doing it someplace else. But doing what? Time was running out, and I was running the risk of being voted most likely to become a burden on society by the same high school intellectuals who tagged me with the nickname "Pisstank," not because I was one but because I looked like one. And like the ad says, you never get a second chance to make a first impression. But screw 'em. I was going to do something with my life ... I just didn't know what.

So I decided to see my guidance counsellor. Guidance counsellors, God love 'em. Are there any good ones? I bet you there are thousands of really good guidance counsellors, but they're not guidance counsellors. Know why? Because their guidance counsellor advised them NOT to be guidance counsellors.

And now I was off to see mine: Mr. Stanley Dudka. A tall, reedy kind of guy, the kind of guy you didn't really want to talk to unless you had to. And I had to. I barged into his office, sat down in front of his desk, looked him straight in the eye and said, "OK, Mr. Dudka, here's the deal. I'm seventeen years old. I'm about to graduate from high school. I'm Jumpy and I don't know what to do with the rest of my life. Can you help?"

Mr. Dudka looked at me, made a few notes, opened a couple of drawers, looked through a few files, made a few more notes, looked at me again and said, "We'll get back to you."

A week later, I still hadn't heard from him. Finally, I spotted him in the hall. I flagged him down.

"Mr. Dudka, Mr. Dudka, what about the rest of my life…?"

"Oh yes, oh yes, oh yes, of course. We've been giving your situation a lot of thought and we think the best thing for you to do is to go to Edmonton for a three-week assessment." When I asked him what exactly did he mean by an assessment, he just looked at me, smiled, patted me on the shoulder and said, "Don't worry, it'll be good for you."

Don't get me wrong. I was about to be a high school graduate, so I had a vague idea what the word meant. But just to be on the safe side, I consulted a dictionary. "Assessment: to assess, to put a value on." Well, that didn't sound so bad. It might even be useful. In the future, if some one came up to me and asked, "Hey, buddy, what's your value?" I could tell 'em. It could be a real bonus.

So my mother packed my bag with jeans and T-shirts and a toothbrush. And my father's 1954 Philishave: two rotary heads, one of which didn't work and the other which spun about as fast as this.

Makes movement.

It didn't so much shave as it plucked … such was my fall from grace.

So now I was off to my assessment, to be assessed … by an assessor. It all has a strangely sexual sound to it, doesn't it? Like, "Hi, I'm Bambi, and I'll be assessing you for three weeks." Yeah, like that's going to happen.

I won't tell you which agency was performing this assessment. Let's just say they had a lot of "Good will." There were three other guys in my assessment group: Louie, a recovering Acidhead; Freddy, a blind guy, and Otto. I never quite figured out Otto's problem, but he used to grin a lot like he knew something I didn't, which I didn't want to know in the first place.

The first week consisted of a series of tests, the first being a big wooden box filled with hundreds of nuts and bolts, which was dumped out in front of me. The task was to find the right nuts that matched the right bolts, attaching them, and then sorting them according to size and shape. I broke out in a cold sweat, flashing back to the horrors of my Meccano set. This and the added pressure of having to compete against my colleagues made me suspect that my sisters must have planned this all.

Otto, the guy with the grin, was amazing. The style and grace and speed with which he put those nuts and bolts together was truly something to behold. I know Otto must be working for Stockwell Day and the Canadian Alliance right now because he just loved twisting things to the right. Louie, the Acidhead, wasn't bad either, but every now and then he would stop and contemplate the bolt and the essence of the nut. . . . Nonetheless, both those guys were done and out of there within half an hour. Me, I took all morning. In fact, I attached my last nut to my last bolt and sorted it successfully at precisely 11:47. But I didn't feel too bad … I did beat the blind guy by a good eight, ten minutes. It was then I learned that in this life, you take your victories where you find them.

Next, we were all taken down to the workshop for two weeks of hands-on meaningful work experience: you take a paper bingo card. You fold it in half. You put the bingo card inside an envelope. You seal the envelope. Do this for 6.5 hours a day, five days a week, and you have your meaningful work experience.

At the time, we all thought this was, to put it politely, Bullshit. Except for Louie. Louie was getting off on the glue.

Finally, after three weeks, we were all called in for the results of our assessment. Top floor to the right. As we waited in the waiting room, I sorta felt like a character from the Wizard of Oz, hoping somebody would tell me how to get whatever it was I was lacking .

Finally, my name was called and I entered a huge office where an elderly woman sat behind a stack of files. The grand assessor. She pulled out my file, read it, Ah ha, ah ha, ah ha … then sniffed

Sniffs and mimics the Grand Assessor.

"Well, Mr. Albert, after an extensive three-week assessment of your skills, it's our determination that you can do anything."

So far, so good. I waited for more. She looked at me as if I hadn't understood.

"Mr. Albert, you can do anything."

"And?"

"You can do anything."

"Is that it?"

"Mr. Albert, it says right here you can do anything!!!! Now, get out of here and go do it!"

"Okay, you don't have to tell me twice."

I thanked her for all her good will and left. Outside in the waiting room, I saw Louie, Freddy and Otto. As I bid them farewell, I could see in their faces that they had just been told that they could do something, but not anything.

On the Greyhound back home, I began to ponder what it all

meant. When I arrived, my parents eagerly asked me what I'd found out, what I'd learned.

"Well, Mom, Dad, I learned that I can stuff bingo cards into envelopes."

Mom and Dad glanced at each other, then nervously sipped their tea. It was obvious that wasn't what they had been hoping to hear.

But I wasn't ready to let the cat out of the bag … not just yet.

Slowly starts putting on shaving cream.

After all, it's a little overwhelming being told you can do anything. Especially after thinking all your life that you could only do something.

Gets more manic with shaving cream.

I'd have to think about this, give it some real thought. Study all the angles. News like this can't be taken lightly. Give me fifteen, twenty minutes … and I'll get back to you.

Ends up with way too much shaving cream on face.

Blackout.

ACT TWO

Vic appears dressed in a casual suit and wearing shades, looking more polished.

Vic: "Hiya, how ya doing? Good, that's real good to hear. So, what can I do for you today? Just looking? That's good, just look. I'm here." *Pause.* "Hey, what do you think about this two-tone job here? Nice, eh? Just got it in but I'll tell you something: it won't be here long. No, no, noooo. Been getting lots of calls on it, lots of calls." *Pause.* "Eight, the boss wants eight. Good deal, eight. But just between you and me, I think you could have it for seven five. You could drive it away for seven five. Oh, you're just looking around. Look around. I'm here." *Pause.* "You know, I think you could take it away for seven four ... maybe even ... seven three. Yeah, yeah, yeah. So ... wanna go for a little spin? Wait here, I'll go and get the keys. Wait here. No, no, no. You're going to drive. You wait here."

Turns to exit to get keys, then turns back to the customer.

"Hey! Where you going? ...See ya..."

Waves.

To audience.

So welcome to my first crack at anything ... automobile salesman. Now I know what you're thinking, but you have to remember this: I was an automobile salesman in a small town—the lowest of the low. Sunshine Motors, owned and operated by my cousin Claude. I had worked for Claude the previous summer washing cars. So when I asked for the job back the next summer, he suggested that instead of washing cars, I should sell them. Wow, the thought of trading in wet clothes, soggy shoes and a sore back for clean clothes, my own office and a swivel chair sounded so sweet. Not only that, I would also be trading in three bucks an hour washing cars for selling them on commission. Could the future be any brighter? I asked Claude to share with me the tricks of the trade, you know, the art of the deal. He took me aside and said, "The one thing you gotta remember is that people will either buy a car or they won't." Then he got into his brand new Cadillac and drove off. The truth of that statement would come back to haunt me many times over the course of the summer.

It's not that I was such a bad salesman; it's just the product was all wrong. I mean, I'm in Bonnyville, Alberta, and Sunshine Motors is a Toyota dealership. It's not that people in small towns dislike Toyotas or Hondas or even Hyundais. They might even admire them … but they don't buy them. It all boils down to a question of life's possibilities.

I went to my brother Bob: "Hey, Bob, a brand new Toyota pickup is exactly what you need."

"Nah, you couldn't get fifty sheets of plywood on one of those."

"But Bob, when's the last time you bought fifty sheets of plywood?"

"You're right, but you never know."

Then I tried my dad: "A brand new Toyota pickup is exactly what you need."

"Nah, you couldn't get fifty pigs on that toy."

"But dad, when's the last time you hauled fifty pigs?!"

"Yeah, you're right, but maybe I will … anything's possible."

Needless to say, I didn't sell my dad or my brother a new Toyota pickup. I did, however, salvage the summer by making a $162 commission on the sale of brand new Toyota Tercel to my sister—who was a registered nurse and the only member of the family where neither pigs nor plywood would be a consideration in the purchase of a new vehicle.

Even though I couldn't sell cars, I sure did like 'em. My fascination began early in life. On Christmas Day 1960, at the ripe old age of two days old, I was traveling at 90 miles per hour on a snow-covered ribbon of road from Bonnyville to the bright lights of Edmonton. The reason for this joyride was that there were problems with my birth. As rumors have it, the blood in my veins did not match my mother's, which is somewhat akin to having diesel in a gas motor. The machine wasn't working.

So there I was, speeding off to Edmonton to have the bad stuff pumped out and the good stuff pumped in. Along for the ride was my Aunt Yvette, who had volunteered for the trip because my father still had seven other children to take care of and my mother was recovering from her eighth trip to the maternity ward in fifteen years.

And because ambulances were as common as Toyotas in 1960 Bonnyville, I was being driven in a big, black Chevy, owned and operated by Cam Fontaine. I say owned and operated because Cam used the big, black Chevy for business—as the town's one and only undertaker. Now, the thought of driving 90 miles an hour on ice-covered roads with an undertaker behind the wheel would make anybody jumpy. But we made it. Cam Fontaine saved my life —- which was pretty big of him because, after all, it was Christmas and I'm sure he coulda used my business.

If you wanted to get analytical about it, you could say that trip was my first close shave. But, hey, what did I know? I was only two days old and happy to be alive. The synapses may not have been firing properly and the body might have had a definite shim, but I made it. I had arrived.

Now the thing about arriving anywhere is that you're sort of obligated to do something once you get there. I had arrived on a farm, a magical place filled with augers and thrashers, combines and spreaders, pulleys and power take-offs. All designed to rip your arm off in the blink of eye. I knew I couldn't have landed in a better place and was eager to do my part.

Yeah, I'm gonna milk some cows, then I am just gonna plow some fields, then I'm gonna put up some barbed wire fence and then I'm gonna bale some hay, and then I'm gonna have some lunch….

My dad didn't let me do any of those things, really, except maybe have lunch. But other people didn't need to know that. Legitimate farm kids had legitimate excuses; I wasn't about to let mine go to waste.

"So, Mr. Albert, could you explain to me why you've been absent from school the last two days?"

"Yes sir, been hauling grain, that's right, hauling grain. That time of year, you know, my dad needs all the help he can get, hopefully we can get the crop off before she freezes … God willing."

I learned a lot hauling grain. Even today, whenever I bank the 8-ball into the corner pocket, I'm thankful for all the grain I've hauled.

OK, so I wasn't going to be a farmer, which was cool because none of my friends wanted to be farmers, either. Some were even militant about it, making t-shirts and bumper stickers that read: "Just say no to summer fallow" and "My other vehicle is NOT a John Deere."

No, this was 1980 and farming was way out. All my friends wanted to be plugged into the oil patch—where anybody with two legs, two arms and a place to hang a hard hat could aspire to the exalted title of rig pig. And who could blame them? Where

else could you make ten thousand bucks an hour, drive to
Edmonton for the weekend in a gold-plated 4x4, blow a million
dollars on booze and drugs and women, lose about a billion
brain cells and come back to work Monday morning, better
equipped for the job.

It did sound like fun, but the oil patch wasn't for me. I was to
soon discover my own little gold mine: The University of Alberta
and my second crack at Anything. Not that I had a burning
desire to go university, and not that I had the academic muscle
either. I had just managed to squeeze out a 56.8 per cent average
in my last year of high school. But what the hell, it seemed as
good as place as any to camp out for four years and try anything.
So I filled out an application with the same naive optimistic-pes-
simism you have when you apply for a Visa card without a job:
hey, all they say is no.

On the phone.

"Yes, I'm calling about my university application ... yes, I realize
that my marks aren't as good as they should be ... yes, you could
say they stink. Oh gee, that's too bad ... oh by the way, but did I
mention that I was ... jumpy. I didn't? Well, I am, I'm very
jumpy. Does that make a difference? Oh. Ohh. Oohhhhhh ... All
right! I guess I'll see you in September then. Well, cum laude to
you, too."

That was it. I was in. Only problem was, once again, no money.
I began filling out application forms for every conceivable student-
financing program under the sun. And on every one, I highlighted
in bold letters, the word, JUMPY. I even filled out the forms by
hand to prove the point. I figured this shotgun approach would
mean at least one would come through to fulfill my destiny as
a University of Alberta student ... but, alas, not a single one
materialized—they all did.

So on September 4th, 1980, I entered the U of A with more income
than someone coming out of university would ever hope to

make … well, someone with an English and drama degree anyway. But with any cheques, there are balances. Six months into my windfall, it was determined by the powers that be that maybe fifteen hundred bucks a month was a tad too generous for a first-year university student.

But it was fun while it lasted. Which pretty well sums up living in Alberta in the early eighties. But even though my financial wings were clipped, as it were, U of A was great. Met a lot of people, made a lot friends … like Petracella.

Petracella Kyrsynowski was a girl with her whole life planned out—until something better came up. She was a political science major working toward a PhD in international relations which she would parlay into a job at the United Nations and over the course of time become a diplomat in some exotic locale where she would inevitably meet and fall in love with an aristocrat and make many baby aristocrats. But right now, she was in a first-year philosophy course with me: Understanding—Understanding 202.

Since we shared the last class of the day, Petracella and I and other like-minded individuals would retire to the nearest coffee shop and discuss why the prof didn't know what the hell he was talking about and we did, being first-year philosophy students. These little tête-à-têtes went on all semester, until one night after a particularly lively discussion on why the Soviet Union would never abandon Communism, Petracella and I found ourselves alone, together. Seeing that we both had term papers due the next day, we decided to have another coffee. It was then that Petracella put her hand on mine and said, "I understand." Not knowing what she meant, I said, "That's great, you'll probably get a good mark, then."

Back in her apartment with absolutely no thoughts of looming term papers, Petracella and I were on the couch. We kissed and then she handed me this.

Pulls out a packaged condom.

As I held it in my hand, I was filled with complete and utter dread. I've had a lot of experience with things like this. The curse of the vacuum wrap. All my life, I've been tormented by these little wonders of packaging: creamers and catsup pouches and little containers of strawberry jam, all designed to take forever to open. Then, when you do, the contents are guaranteed to go everywhere except where you want them to. But, I've adapted: I drink my coffee black, I eat fries with just a touch of salt. However, in this situation, I had to get the jam on the toast. I knew if I fiddled with it too long, the very reason for opening it would be long gone. Petracella sensed my dilemma; she took the package from my hand and said once again, "I understand." And she did.

Petracella and I understood each other a couple more times that semester, until she dropped out of university the next term. I guess something better came up. I don't know where she went or if she's doing what she wanted or even if she found her aristocrat. I hope so. Seeing nothing better came up for me, I hung in at university, which was fine, except I didn't get to understand anybody else. And after four years I was finally prepared for the real world.

"Okay, all you employers who want to throw big money at someone who's just finished university with an arts degree in English and drama, line up here! Don't push, don't panic. I'll get to everyone of you in due time."

So maybe I wasn't as prepared as I thought. But I needed to do something, so I took refuge in the last hope of the chronically under employed: I became a writer—my third crack at Anything. And the miraculous thing about being a writer is that you don't necessarily have to have written anything to call yourself one … well, for the first five years anyway.

I started hanging out at the Media Club in Edmonton. The Media Club, if you haven't had the pleasure, is a place where writers and producers and actors go and talk. And seeing that I was a newly self-ordained writer, The Media Club seemed like a ideal place to hang and learn all about the biz. It was there I was to make a very a good friend who would have a big influence on my new career ... ladies and gentlemen, allow me to introduce my good buddy, *pulls out beer can.* Beer. I had been acquainted with, *indicates beer can,* at one time or another, but at the Media Club, we became real pals.

My friend helped me with my pool game, my dating game—"hey, baby"—and just about any other game you can imagine ... because when, *holds up beer,* is around, I don't feel jumpy. Go figure. With a beer in my hand, I've walked tightropes, I've juggled chain saws, I've built entire cities out of Meccano ... or at least I think I did.

But as everyone knows, when drinking beer over the course of an evening, or a life time, you run across something called the First Law of Diminishing Returns, which simply states that whatever gains you have made, perceived or otherwise, through the consumption of six beers, you will lose them immediately on the consumption of the seventh. Not only that, you will not be aware of this loss.

This law dovetails nicely into my own personal theory of the Universal Anecdote. The universal anecdote is a story that we all have ... and it's always about someone we've never met before. It always begins like this: "Did I ever tell you about this goof I met dot dot dot." From there, we go on to explain how this person made a complete ass of himself in our presence. We all have this story, and because we all have this story, it stands to reason that at some point in our life, we become "the goof" in somebody else's story. Some of us, however, are in more stories than others.

Now, I had been hanging out at the Media Club a lot in my quest for anything. And I soon discovered that the Media Club was a place where writers went to talk about scripts they'd never write, where producers went to talk about films they'd never produce, and where actors went to talk and to talk and to talk....

One particular Friday night, I cruised into the Media Club about seven o'clock to enjoy the evening of mirth and merriment with Edmonton's media elite—both of them. After several hours, it was time to go home. I made my way up the stairs and on to the street. Outside, three young men were standing smoking. I smiled, said goodnight and started on home. It was then I heard one of them say, "Boy, oh boy, is that guy ever drunk."

I stopped in my tracks. Usually, I tend to ignore these pedestrian comments. But that night, I felt the need, the moral obligation, to make a stand. I turned on my heel and walked back to the pack. "Listen, pal, I'm not drunk, I was born this way. And if you've got a problem with that, that's your problem 'cause I'm just trying to live my life!"

The look on their faces, you could've sworn that I'd just caught them spitting on the Pope. They tried to stammer out an apology, but I held my ground ... glaring at them ... making them feel this small ... making them think I was capable of anything. And I was ... and then ... and then ... *Beat* ... I threw up.

The next morning, I woke up with a raging hangover. I stumbled out of bed thinking that food might be the answer. What better way to relieve post-party depression than a refreshing bowl of Cheerios. Cheeerrioooos. But instead of seeing whole-grain toasty o's floating cheerfully in a bowl of a milk, I saw hundreds of zeros adrift on an unforgiving sea of white and I realized that I was one of those zeros, just waiting to drown in my own stupidity and indifference.

I had gone over the line, not that throwing up in public is anything to get all choked up about. No, what was bothering me was the timing of it all. There I was for the first time in my life ready to make a stand, to tell the world what I thought, what I really believed, and what did I end up doing? I ended up giving three guys a story that begins, "Did I ever tell you about this goof I met dot dot dot." Not good, definitely not good.

The irony was too heavy. So heavy I had to get out, get some air, get some distance ... do something ... do anything. I walked and I walked and I walked. Up and down streets I've never walked down before. Finally, I found myself walking down a street where a man was washing windows. As I approached him, he stopped what he was doing, and began to stare ... at me. I was in no mood for another confrontation, so I bowed my head and walked on past.

"Hey, I know you!"

I turned and looked and I saw the grin. "Otto?"

It was Otto. "Hey, Otto, long time no see, how's it been going!?"

"Ahh, it's been OK, you know, been doing things, working here, working there, but I got my own business now. I know it's only washing windows ... but what the hell, I started with one, and now, I'm doing the whole street. I got my own trapline!"

"That's really great, Otto." He asked me what I had been up to.

I didn't really want to get into it, so I said, "I'm doing nuthin."

"Hope it pays well, anyway gotta get back to work. Gotta finish up the job." It was then that he caught my reflection in the window. He turned to me and grew an extra large grin. "You know something Vic, you should really shave, you look like shit!" Then he picked up his pail of water and trudged off down the street.

Pause.

I walked home ... and locked myself in the bathroom.

Sprays shaving cream on hand, studies it for a moment, then applies it to face. Picks up razor and begins to shave until done.

Thirty-seven minutes later, I emerged clean shaven—not a nick, not a scratch, no cuts, no blood. Nothing. I had done it.
I had conquered my face and on my own terms.

Until the next time and the next time and the next. Like Sisyphus and his rock, I knew I would have to do this over and over and over again. There's no turning back. And like anything you have to do over and over and over, you get complacent—which leads to carelessness, which leads to little scraps of bloody toilet paper all over your face.

But you don't care. You know you have the patience, the concentration, and the co-ordination to do a good job. What's a little blood, anyway? I mean how much damage can you do, just scraping the surface ... everything heals ... eventually. That's life....

But then again, there are always those who will embark on heroic pursuits in order to feel alive ... some bungy jump, some race automobiles, some leap from skyward planes. I ... *pulls out a straight razor, holds it to face* ... shave.

Blackout.

Lyle Victor Albert in *Objects in Mirror are Stranger Than They Appear.*
Photo by The Edmonton Journal.

Objects in Mirror

are stranger

than they appear

Objects in Mirror … Are Stranger Than They Appear was first produced at the Saskatoon Fringe Festival in July 1997, with Richard Lett as director. Other productions were at the Edmonton Fringe, August 1997; The High Performance Rodeo (One Yellow Rabbit) in Calgary, January 1998; The UNO festival, Victoria, February 1998; and Vancouver Comedy Festival, July 1999.

Lights UP: Vic on the telephone.

Vic: "C'mon honey, can't we talk … I just want to talk … that's all…. Can't we? What d' you mean there's nothing to talk about … there's tons. Well, we could talk about me … I'm kidding … You know I'm kidding … Well, I am kidding. All I'm saying is that we should talk … Don't hang up. Honey, How can I listen when I'm trying to make you talk? OK that was a stupid thing to say. OK, fine, I'm stupid. I'm the stupidest guy on earth, OK? NOW can we talk? Don't hang up … don't you dare, I'm warning you. This is the last time you will ever hang up … on me."

Vic begins loading boxes in his "car." SFX: "You ain't seen nothin yet."

Goodbye. See ya later, colour me outta here. Gone. Hasta la vista. Bye bye. Elvis has left the building and he's taking me with him.

Relationships, relationships. RE-LA-TION-SHIPS. Four little syllables that mean so much and ultimately nothing at all. Let's define it, shall we?

RE as in pertaining to, or a prefix denoting repetition, as in Let's talk about Where Our Relationship Is Going, over and over again.

Which brings us to LA, as in LA, the note that follows "Sooooo, honey, does it have to go anywhere? I mean it's not like it has wheels." This lame attempt at humour leads directly to TION, as in I never want to see you again, you jerk!

Which finally brings us to SHIP, as in a means of transport. The jerk with no witty comeback to "I NEVER WANT TO SEE YOU AGAIN." No choice but to ship out, go away, run away.

My ship is a 1986 Honda Civic Hatchback, four speed, 1.3-litre engine. Stronger than a lawn mower, weaker than just about anything else on four wheels. But what it lacks in power, it makes up for in determination, just like me … sort of.

In the back of my Honda are clothes, dishes, books, stereo equipment, television, a computer and anything else that fits. Which it all does. It's a sobering realization to discover that at 38 years old, all of your earthly possessions can fit nicely into … well, a Honda.

Now maybe I'm going a little overboard. I mean, people break up every day and both still manage to live in the same city, neighbourhood or even apartment block. But not me, no way, because I tend to be a little bit indecisive … sort of….

So I'm gonna make distance make the decision for me. Time to hit the highway. I LOVE that word, highway. You can stay on your low way, but I'm on the highway.

Departure: the prairies, Edmonton, Alberta. Destination: The Coast. Vancouver, British Columbia.

The land of mild winters, hard bodies and good drugs. Now, many people refer to B.C. as "Bring Cash." But I have an ace in the hole. I've got three months left on an unemployment claim and a place to crash for two weeks. It's the Canadian dream, and I'm living it.

Begins to drive. SFX: "Car Jamming."

Now the thing that amazes me whenever I'm behind the wheel of a car is that *Beat*. I'm behind the wheel of a car. I'm in control of half a tonne of metal, rubber and combustible fuel, going maybe 100, 110 clicks per hour. It's a frightening thought, but I had no choice.

TRANSITION, LIGHTING AND MUSIC

Way back in 1913, Tomas Albert decided to make a move: the unsettled West was beckoning with the promise of cheap land and a better life. His mother, however, felt Tomas was being foolhardy.

"Why go all the way there, when you have enough right here." But the lure of wealth and freedom was too great, so Tomas loaded himself on to a train. "Au revoir, maman," and headed thataway—all the way to Bonnyville, Alberta, to his new 130-acre parcel of bush. TABERNAC!

Over the years, the bush became a farm complete with a wife, 12 children. TABERNAC! In 1946, the fourth son of Tomas took over the farm. He and his wife raised eight children, seven farm kids and me, desperately wondering: HOW THE HELL AM I GOING TO GET OFF THIS PLACE?? Because when you grow up on a farm, your world is defined by where you can walk to and when you're three years old and you're just beginning to walk (Hey, I'm just going by me), that world is immense and wonderful. A trip to the chicken coop could take an hour, going to the pig pen, the better part of the morning, and to the hay stack, pack a lunch.

But once you get a little older, chicken coops, pig pens and haystacks all have a distinctive been-there, done-that feel to them. I knew I had to escape.

Transition with lighting. SFX: "Blue Skies."

Edson, Alberta, and my resolve is stronger than ever. As I'm filling the tank, I see the woman behind the counter checking me out. Maybe she's wondering if I'm actually driving. Maybe she just wants ME.

I am making the right decision—which is a feat for someone who's indecisive … sort of. Besides, what's the alternative? Gave up my apartment, said goodbye to all my friends, got no job … and she's there. She didn't think I'd go. God knows, I threatened enough. I'm outa here … then I'd get scared. Then, "Honey, it's me, can we talk?" And then the whole cycle would begin again. Well, no more. It's finished! I've finally pulled the plug and all I can say is, "Darling, if the phone doesn't ring, it's me."

Transition with lighting

By the time I was nine, I had the walking thing pretty much down. It was time to get some wheels into the act. I was bound and determined to learn to ride a bicycle. Not that it was an easy sell to my parents. I started around June: "Mom, can I have a bike?"

"No, it's too dangerous."

A few days later, "Mom, can I have a bike?"

"No, you'll hurt yourself!"

A few days later, "Mom, I want a bike!"

"Go ask your father."

Hmmm, I was making headway.

By the time October rolled around, I knew I was breaking my parents' will. I wasn't getting a flat "no" any more. Nor was I being played between Mom and Dad. Now it was, "We'll see," "If you're good," or "I'll get you a damn bike if you'd just stop bugging me." It all paid off at Christmas that year.

Vic brings bike on stage.

It wasn't new, the paint was badly chipped and the seat was held together with electrical tape. But so what? It had two wheels and it was all mine. My bike. A banana bike! And I couldn't wait to take it for a spin. One problem: Christmas in Alberta, 40 below and five feet of snow.

So in between December and God knows when Spring will come, all I could do was go out to our unheated garage and sit on my bike … and sit and sit. Because I knew, instinctively, that if I sat on my bike in a sub-zero garage for hours on end, the Bicycle Gods would give me the big thumbs-up when the snow finally left. I would fling open the garage door and ride out ... in a blaze of glory.

Unfortunately, the Bicycle Gods have no jurisdiction on a farm where there's not a smooth surface in sight. No Bicycle Gods here and you're on your own to deal with the dirt, the mud, the long grass and loose gravel. Oh well, no one said escape, let alone balance, would be easy.

Vic attempts to ride the bike.

Hey, look at that, that was at least five feet. Slowly but surely, I began to master my new ship, and by the end of August I was riding my bike ... I was even going out on the road, exploring, seeing the world out on my own. I'd go for miles and miles. I was off the farm and I was free at last ... and then it snowed ... again.

Transition with lighting. SFX: "Do you feel loved."

C'mon, c'mon, c'mon, Jesus will you move that thing, 45 miles an hour, I don't believe it CAAAAMOOOOON.

Fifteen minutes out of Jasper I come upon something humongous and immovable and it's not the Rockies. It's a Winnebago, an Indian word meaning Slow-Moving One Taking Much Room. WE'RE SPENDING OUR KIDS' INHERITANCE. Well, bully for you, mom and dad, but I say give it to the brats. At least they'll buy a faster vehicle with it. God, I could use a smoke.

SHE never liked me to smoke, especially when I was driving.

"You can't smoke and drive."

"Of course I can, it's not against the law ... yet."

"No, YOU can't smoke and drive. You always drop it on your pants, on your shirt. I've seen the burn holes."

"Bullshit. It's battery acid. I got that overhauling my … uh … a computer".

"You should quit for your own good."

For my own good. At first, I didn't mind when she said it. It felt … good. She cared, and I did quit … for her. But by then, "for my own good" meant not hanging around with my friends so much, not drinking so much, not being … me … so much. All for my own good.

But I guess, somewhere down the road, for my own good wasn't good enough.

TRANSITION, lighting and music

It's amazing: what was once a great accomplishment when you're nine fades into relentless tedium now that you're thirteen. By that time, you and your bike know every dip, every hill, every mudhole, every pothole, every curve, on every road for miles around. And you have to face facts: the magic is gone.

Now the magical thing about magic is that you never know when it's going to appear. It might be something you've seen for years, taken for granted, then one day—holy shit.

There it was, our 1965 Dodge Fargo half-ton. It wasn't much to look at; dented and rusty, scraped and scarred from years of hauling grain, pigs and shit. But now, for the first time, I saw its inner beauty, its hidden charms.

My brothers had driven it. So had my sisters. I figured it was my turn. My Dad had other ideas: No! Months went by, I was sick and tired of waiting for him to give me the green light….

The right time was Sunday morning, church time, and the only time when I could be guaranteed a hour undisturbed with the Fargo. And, as luck would have it, the very next Sunday I developed the severest case of stomach cramps ever. "Mom, I can't go to church. I'm sick."

Usually, you had to produce your own death certificate before you were excused from church, but by some miracle, she bought it. All right!

As soon as I saw the family car cruise down the driveway, I was up and out, heading for Fargo. A thousand butterflies were doing the rumba in my belly as I slipped my key into her ignition. It felt good. It felt real good.

Vic starts the motor.

Brumm, brumm, bruuuuummmmm. O God. I think I'm going to faint. I composed myself. Let's see, the thing you gotta do is give it a lot of gas ... BRUUMMMMMMM ... and let go of the clutch really fast ... or was it the other way around?

The back wheels tore into the earth like demons from hell. I froze, including the foot that rested on the gas pedal. Holy Shit! All I could do is try my best to steer the beast out of harm's way. Suddenly, the beast swung around with fury, making a beeline for what it craved—our five hundred gallon tank of gasoline. Ohhhh my Gooooood. My feet sprang to life, flailing like mad, looking for any pedal that would make the bad machine stop.

Vic hits the brake.

The truck skidded for what seemed like an eternity. The front bumper caught one of the metal posts holding up the tank, causing it to buckle, causing the tank to teeter back and forth ever so slowly until ... it finally took the plunge ... it bounced off the roof of the truck, landing next to it like a huge metallic beach ball.

I guess I should have been grateful that gas tank was nearly empty, but grateful was the last thing I was feeling ... Now I really was sick. All I could hope for was that the sermon at church had been all about forgiveness.

Transition with lighting. SFX: "Pretty Woman"

Somewhere between Clearwater and Blue River, I need to …
turns to pee. Oh man, six hours on the road and I'm not even half
way there yet. Maybe I should phone her, you know, just to tell …
her I'm all right. I'm on the road and I'm all right. I'm in the middle of nowhere … anything could happen to me out here, she
might be worried, maybe … maybe she'd just hang up. No phone
around here anyway, nothing around here. Oh, well, no use even
thinking about it. It's beginning to rain … just me and the rain.

Transition with lighting.

You know you've done something so insanely stupid when your
family won't even acknowledge how insanely stupid it is. There's
no anger, no yelling, no gnashing of teeth. There's just that unend-
ing and excruciating silence. The type of silence that sucks the
air out of the room and leaves you gasping.

Everyone was already seated at the table for Sunday dinner when
I finally had the courage to come downstairs. No one even looked
up from their plates so I sat down at my spot and asked, "So how
was church?" If looks could kill, I would have died nine times that
sunny Sunday.

The next day that wall of silence was in no danger of tumbling
down. My father quietly went about the business of fixing the
tank stand, putting the tank back on it and trying to repair the
new dents on the truck the best he could. Me? I was keeping the
lowest of the low profiles. Finally, my father came into the house
and announced he was going into town … and he was taking me
with him.

The silence was broken immediately after I got in the truck.
Braaroooom. It's amazing how much my dad sounded like the
Dodge Fargo in times like these. He continued for thirteen miles
into town and twelve miles back. A mile from the farm, Dad
stopped the truck. Oh boy, I guess this is where he's going to
bury the body. Dad got out of the truck and walked around to
the passenger door. Then he said, "I want you to drive home."

What? Was this a trick? Some sort of demented reverse double-whammy?

He wasn't kidding. And I slid over behind the wheel, my heart pounding.

"All right. The first thing you have to learn is letting the clutch out slowly and giving it gas slowly."

Begins to jerk forward.

"Give it more gas. Keep on the right side of the road. All right now. Use the clutch and shift into second."

This time it was remarkably smooth. "More gas." The engine now demanded its third gear, and I obliged it. Wow, this is fun. I was about to give the engine its fourth gear, when Dad said, "Slow down!" The mile was almost over and it was time to turn in the yard.

Oh man, I was just getting going and now it was about to end. Well, not quite. I still had to slow down. I pushed in the clutch and begin to shift back to second. But I didn't find second. I found fourth, and the truck wasn't letting up. "Use your brake!" The turn into the driveway was upon us, but I was determined we were going to make it. So I slammed on the brakes and turned the wheel. Just like Starsky and Hutch. But I wasn't Starsky and my father wasn't Hutch, and the Dodge Fargo certainly wasn't a Grand Torino. What we were … was in the ditch.

Transition with lighting. SFX: "Fields of Gold"

Dumb, Dumb, dumb. I don't want the No. One. I want the No. Five, the Coquihalla. Stupid, Stupid. Now I gotta turn around, backtrack. Shit. I wasn't paying attention … again. That's what she would always say: "you never pay attention." Pay attention to what? Pay attention to yourself. Look in the mirror. What do you want? I want you, you know that. I don't know that. You only want to be with me when you have no other place else to go. You expect me to be here for you. It's strange. No, what's strange is that you are always there. Why don't you look in the mirror, what's your problem? *Pause.* Well, if you're not happy, maybe you should find somebody else. I don't want somebody else. *Pause.* There is no one else.

Transition, music and lighting.

After hitting the ditch, I swore that I'd never get behind the wheel again. Who needs it? I mean, millions of people don't drive, and they're happy, aren't they? Well, aren't they? And I don't care if I never get off this farm. I love this place.

I went to my father to tell him of my resolve. I thought he'd be relieved. But he smiled and said, "Don't be afraid of your mistakes. You'll learn."

And I did. Out in the hay fields. Where there's room for mistakes. I learned to shift up, to shift down, to turn, and to brake. I even learned to parallel park between hay bales. Now it was time to make it legal, time to get my driver's licence. No problem. No worries.

The Department of Motor Vehicles ... Now there's a bunch of worrywarts. I think the whole organization began developing some serious grey hairs when I walked into their office and announced, "HI. I'm here to take my driver's test."

Now that's what I thought I said, but judging by the expression of the man behind the counter, I might have said, Hi, I'm a Martian and I'm here to impregnate your daughter.

"I'm sorry son, I can't let you take a driver's test, not until you get this filled out."

A medical? Hey, I'm not sick. Aaaah man, after weeks of studying the Motor Vehicles Handbook, learning every rule of the road backwards and forwards, knowing that this means left and this means right ... *does incorrect arm gestures for turn signals* ... It's the other way around ... knowing all this and still to come away with a sheet of paper that asks, Have you ever been a drug addict?

Date of birth: December 23, 1960. Height: Five feet, five and one-half inches. Weight: 125 pounds. Sex: Maybe, once I get a driver's licence.

Epilepsy NO.
Narcolepsy NO.
Extreme obesity NO.
Psychopathic Personality NO.

Piece of cake. This was just a formality, a safety check done by people who need to do something. But nestled in between Parkinson's Disease and Chronic Heart Condition were two words: Cerebral Palsy.

Hey, is that a problem? I had never heard that term before. Sure, sure, I knew I was different, but I didn't know it had a name—and I'm 16 years old. Either people thought I couldn't handle the truth or I really did grow up in the bush. The doctor looked at me: "This is a problem."

Cerebral Palsy is caused, more often than not, by a seizure at birth—not the drink, the medical kind. There is always the risk another seizure will occur later in life, which would be a drag if you were behind the wheel. The test to detect if a seizure will happen again is called an Electroencephalograph, which, if you can pronounce it, you don't need it. An electroencephalograph is painless, but you must remain totally motionless.

Transition with lighting. SFX: "Out On The Tiles"

The Coquihalla: expect sudden weather changes. No kidding. The wind came out of nowhere, and I can feel it push me. It does down for a moment and then another gust. It's a little tricky keeping the Honda on track ... but it's nothing I can't handle. Everybody goes through this. I'm no different.

Transition with lighting.

"All right, Mr. Albert. We will begin the test now. Just relax and remain completely still."

Begins to shake

"You're moving."

"Am I? Sorry. How's this?"

Still shakes.

"You're still moving!"

"So I am."

"Mr. Albert, if you can't complete this test, I can't approve your medical."

Transition with lighting. SFX: "Out On The Tiles"

As if the wind wasn't bad enough, now it's raining, really coming down hard. It's getting a little tough to see. But hey, it's not that bad. She wasn't right for me. Accept it. I'll find somebody else. I just got to believe it.

Transition with lighting.

"I can do this. I can." But the worry is making my body even more out of control. Out of the corner of my eye I see the doctor. His face says it all. This kid's not going to make it.

Transition with lighting., SFX: "Out On The Tiles"

Snow. It's snowing. And you have to PAY to be on this? All right, you're from Alberta. You grow snow. Deal with it. *Another gust.* The wind seems to be getting stronger. Why did she put up with me? She's right, it's strange, I'm strange. Why would anyone put up with me?

Transition with lighting.

The doctor tries to explain. Perhaps it wouldn't be in my best interest to drive.

"But doc, I can ride a bike. I can drive a truck. I can parallel park between hay bales."

"That's all right on a farm, but in the outside world, you run the risk of hurting yourself or other people. Just be content with what you can do."

Transition with lighting., SFX: "Out On The Tiles"

ICE. I can feel it beneath my tires. The back end's sliding. Use your brake. No don't use your break. Way to go, Starsky. She accepted me, isn't that what I wanted. But wasn't good enough for me. Who the hell do I think I am? What makes me think that I can choose?

Transition with lighting.

"Doc. Please, can't we give it another try. I'll do better this time...." "Just relax and remain motionless ... try concentrating on the beating of your heart." Good idea. Concentrate on the beating of your heart. BA BUM ... BA BUM ... BA BUM ... BA BOOM!

Transition with lighting., SFX: "Out On The Tiles"

The Honda's in a skid ... do you turn into a skid or out? In? Out? Son of a bitch, make a decision! Do something! I crank on the wheel ... gee, I'm going sideways, doing 360s ... once, twice ... and then, stop. *Touching his heart.* Holy Shit. Any damage? I feel OK. I'm alive I think. The Honda seems to be OK. Maybe if I go a little slower, I can get out of this.

The car is stuck.

Stuck. AAAAHHH.

Gets out of car, slips, reads sign.

Avalanche area. Do not stop. What the hell am I doing here? I don't have to be here. Nobody was forcing me to go. I'll work it out, I'll adapt, I'll be content!

BA BUM BA BUM ... Etc.

Vic closes his eyes, his body becomes still. Pause. With effort he pushes his car off the ice, and carefully gets in.

"The results of the electroencephalograph indicate there is no abnormal brain activity, the risk of another seizure is minimal, therefore, there is no medical reason preventing you from obtaining a driver's licence."

Transition with lighting., SFX: "City Girls"

Vic begins to unload boxes from the back of the car.

The day I took my driver's test, the sky was overcast. I wore a purple shirt and my mother cooked pot roast for supper. The reason I recall those details is because that's the day I passed the driver's test—the first time out. Don't ask me what the weather was like when I got my first flat tire, or what I was wearing when I got my first speeding ticket. Or what I'd eaten before I had my first accident. Some firsts are more important than others. And some beginnings are endings, too.

Picks up the phone and dials.

"Hi, it's me ... Don't hang up. I just wanted to say I'm here, Vancouver, British Columbia. It's a beautiful city. I'll send you a postcard. How you doing? Me? Just unpacking my life. Listen, I have to let you go, you know, long distance. I just called to say, take care of yourself. Don't worry about me. I'll be fine. I'll be just fine."

Lights fade to black.

L YLE VICTOR ALBERT was born into a French/Irish Catholic family in 1960, the youngest of eight children. He was raised on a farm near Bonnyville, Alberta, and eventually attended Grant MacEwan Community College in Edmonton, Alberta, where he obtained a diploma in Theatre Production. He also attended the University of Alberta, where he worked on a BA in English and in Drama. Albert has been a playwright in residence, a staff writer for a media company, and a car salesman. Of his many plays, two have been previously published: "The Prairie Church of Buster Galloway" in the *New Works Anthology*, and "*Cut!*" in *Five from the Fringe*.

He currently lives in Radium Hot Springs, B.C. with his partner Beverly Cressman whose love and support is a constant inspiration.